Massachusetts Lighthouses

A Pictorial Guide

Chatham Light, Chatham, MA.

Massachusetts Lighthouses

A Pictorial Guide

Courtney Thompson

Designed, edited and published by
CatNap Publications
Mt. Desert, Maine

ISBN: 0-9651786-5-X
Library of Congress Catalog Card Number: **98-70230**

Photography and editing: Courtney Thompson

Maps and line graphics:
Rusty Nelson, South Portland, Maine

Narrative material:
Jeremy D'Entremont, Winthrop, MA.

Printed in Canada by
Quebecor Atlantic
St. John, New Brunswick
Canada

For purchase information please contact:
CatNap Publications
P.O. Box 848
Mt. Desert, ME. 04660
(207) 244-0485

*For my father. His forethought and love
made this project possible*

Table of Contents

Cape Ann & North Shore to New Hampshire

Salem Shore

Boston Harbor

South Shore

Cape Cod

Cape Cod (Con't)

Southeastern Shore

Martha's Vineyard & Nantucket

Lighthouses of the Past

Introduction

The maritime history of Massachusetts is a vivid one, replete with images and tales of shipwrecks, heroism, pirates and pilgrims. Whaling, fishing and international shipping also were important elements of that history. Lighthouses also were an integral part of the story. The sea and safe passage upon the water were essential to life and times when transportation was primarily by boat and settlement concentrated near and along the coast. Lighthouses offer a tangible reminder of a time when life was of a simpler vein yet in many ways presented more rigorous challenges. During the 18th and 19th centuries lighthouses were the mariners' guide to the waterways, but were always themselves to some degree at the mercy of the sea's power.

Primarily, lighthouses represented safety and certainty to early mariners, reassurance and constant point of reference amid changing seas, unpredictable weather and dangerous journeys. They evoke today a similar sense and strength of purpose. The lights are at once peaceful, lonely, beautiful, forlorn, silent or raucous, signaling both welcome and warning-- subject often to harsh, unforgiving conditions yet in locations of breathtaking beauty. A benevolent appearance under clear skies and calm seas often becomes an aura of foreboding and loneliness brought about by dense fog or a powerful 'noreaster. Lighthouses which host summer visitors, in winter become wonderfully deserted and peaceful; those which in summer offer a challenging, appealing destination for vacationing sailors become isolated and face winter's storms head on.

With advances in navigational tools and techniques it's noted that the technical function of the lighthouse is no longer required. The intangible elements which these structures provide, however, are significant and irreplaceable. This book is intended to offer a comprehensive pictorial tour of the Massachusetts lighthouses. The historic images are included to provide a glimpse into the past, when the lighthouses all were vital, functioning and peopled; dates are noted when possible. Maps and directions give specific routes to and/or sense of location for each beacon. The collection of multiple photographs, historic images, maps, directions and narrative notes into one volume offers a complete look at each lighthouse, hopefully comparable to a "walk" or trip around the grounds.

Completion of this project involved travel over well-known routes, discovery of little-used back roads, and exploration of coves and islands. Many people were gracious in their assistance and I was privileged to gain access to private properties and special locations. Everyone I met during this adventure was helpful, patient, cooperative and encouraging. In particular, Jeremy D'Entremont contributed extensive narrative material gathered for his own lighthouse project, representing hours of research, compilation and writing. Additionally, he graciously allowed use of selected photographs, offering an angle I'd missed or a particularly appealing light situation. Rusty Nelson created the maps included in the book with particular care and expertise. His friendship and advice were invaluable to this effort.

Finally, my thanks to all others who helped me along the way in whatever manner.

Cape Ann & the North Shore to New Hampshire

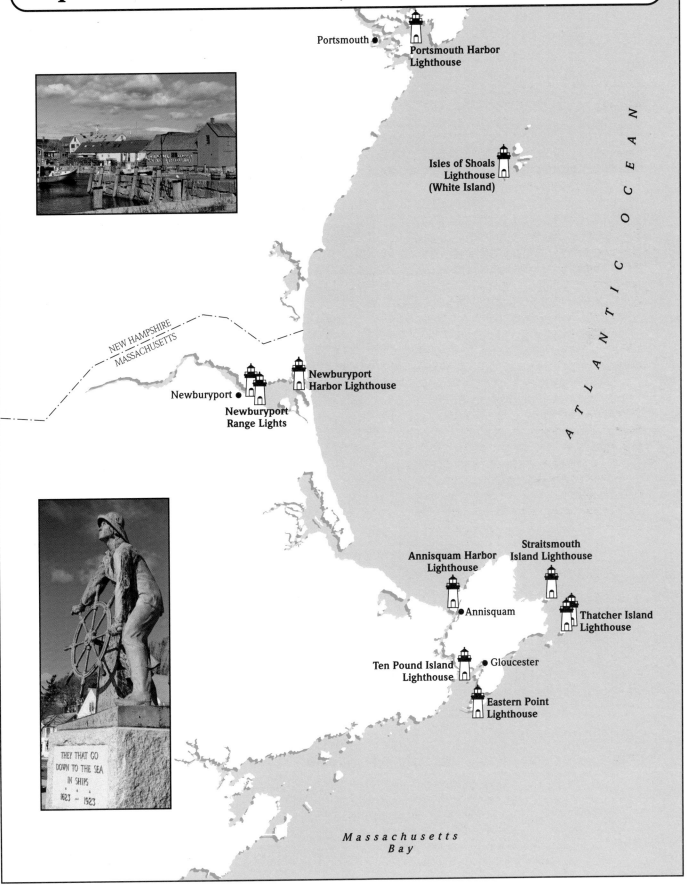

Portsmouth •
**Portsmouth Harbor
Lighthouse**

**Isles of Shoals
Lighthouse
(White Island)**

ATLANTIC OCEAN

NEW HAMPSHIRE
MASSACHUSETTS

**Newburyport
Harbor Lighthouse**

Newburyport •
**Newburyport
Range Lights**

**Annisquam Harbor
Lighthouse**

**Straitsmouth
Island Lighthouse**

• Annisquam

**Thatcher Island
Lighthouse**

**Ten Pound Island
Lighthouse**

• Gloucester

**Eastern Point
Lighthouse**

*Massachusetts
Bay*

THEY THAT GO
DOWN TO THE SEA
IN SHIPS
1623 ~ 1923

Portsmouth Harbor Light

A lantern on a pole was the first "lighthouse" established in 1771 at Ft. William and Mary, a British stronghold on Newcastle Island guarding Portsmouth Harbor. The first overt act of the Revolutionary War occurred in the area in December 1774. After learning of British plans to strengthen the fort, Paul Revere rode to Portsmouth from Boston with the news. Forewarned, the colonists overpowered the fort and made off with supplies.

A more permanent tower was built during the period 1782-1784, making it one of America's twelve colonial lighthouses. Following transfer of

the property to the federal government, President George Washington is said to have visited the lighthouse.

In 1804 a new octagonal wooden tower was constructed and replaced in 1877 with a new 48-foot cast-iron tower; a fourth-order Fresnel lens was installed. The fortifications on Newcastle Island, now attached by causeway to the mainland, became known as Ft. Constitution. Portsmouth Harbor Light was automated in 1960 and is part of the Ft. Constitution Historic Site, adjacent to an active Coast Guard Station.

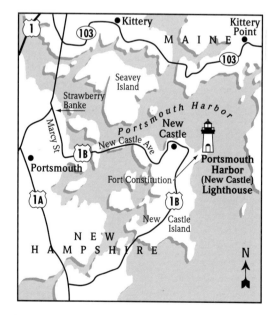

Directions: From I-95 or U.S. Route 1, take the waterfront exit and/or follow the signs to the Strawberry Banke area. Follow Marcy Street (RT 1B) through this area toward Newcastle; the road becomes New Castle Avenue. Continue on 1B into New Castle to Wentworth Avenue. Turn left (Ft. Constitution Historic Site sign), then bear right to the parking area. The light can also be seen in the distance from Ft. McClary in Kittery, Maine.

Isles of Shoals (White Island) Light

White Island is one of nine windswept islands nine miles east of the mouth of the Piscataqua River. First known as the Smythes Isles (discovered by Captain John Smith in 1614), they were renamed by fisherman for plentiful "schools" of fish found in the area. A 17th-century land grant allotted the southern four islands to New Hampshire, the remainder to Maine.

The first Isles of Shoals lighthouse was an 87-foot stone tower established in 1821. White Island's second light, erected in 1859, remains in operation. The tower is a 58-foot cylindrical brick tower with walls two feet thick. This station was automated in 1987 and subsequently converted to solar power.

Severe storms in the fall of 1992 destroyed the fog signal, covered walkways, and other equipment and outbuildings. Nothing was done to replace any of the structures and in 1993 the light station was deeded to the State of New Hampshire. Renovations have since been undertaken. Excursion boats from Portsmouth will go to the Isles of Shoals, but not all go by White Island for close views of the lighthouse.

The light must be photographed by boat; some tour boats from Portsmouth pass closeby.

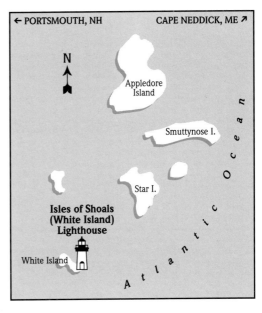

Newburyport Harbor Range Lights

The range lights were first built in 1873 to help mariners entering Newburyport Harbor from the Merrimac River. The Front Range light originally was an octagonal wooden tower located on Bayley's Wharf. The Rear Range light is a 53-foot brick tower with cast-iron lantern room and balcony. The lighthouse is square with some tapering in the midsection.

These lights were discontinued in 1961 and in 1964 the Front Range light was moved to the nearby grounds of a Coast Guard Station. In 1990 it was changed to a more traditional appearance with short, white tower and red and white lantern room. After decommissioning, the Rear Range light was sold to private ownership. Both lights are listed on the National Register of Historic Places.

Rear Range Light

Front Range Light

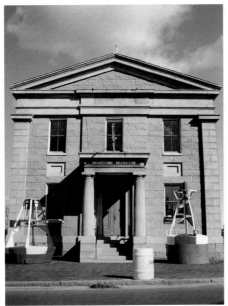

Maritime Museum

Directions:

Newburyport can be reached by taking I-95 to Exit 57 and following Rt. 133 east to "Downtown Newburyport" or via Routes 1 and 1A. Signs indicating the Historic/Downtown area are easily followed. Any of several cross streets will lead to Water Street (Broad, State, Federal are examples). The front range light is located inside the U.S. Coast Guard Merrimack River Station on Water St. between Federal and Tremont streets. Parking is available behind the building. The rear range tower is on Water Street, just south of the Coast Guard Station and is easily identified once in the area.

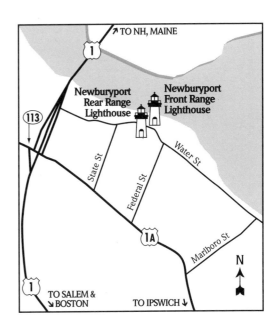

13

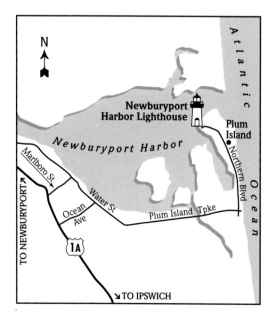

Directions:

From I-95, take Exit 57 (Historic Newburyport) to Rt 113 into Newburyport (or from Rt 1, exit to Downtown Newburyport). Take one of the main cross streets(Broad, Federal, State) north to Water Street (most all cross streets will take you there). Follow Water Street east to a T-intersection with Ocean Avenue. A sign indicating Plum Island & Parker River Refuge is to the left. Continue straight on the Plum Island Turnpike; turn left onto Northern Blvd. and follow this road to its end at the Parker River National Wildlife Refuge.

Or: Take MA 1A North to Newbury. At the first traffic light, turn right onto Ocean Avenue(a "Plum Island" directs you). Follow Ocean Avenue to its end at a T-intersection with Plum Island Turnpike and turn right; there is a sign indicating Parker River Refuge. Follow above directions to the lighthouse.

Newburyport Harbor (Plum Island)Light

Shifting channels at the mouth of the Merrimack River made entrance to Newburyport harbor difficult and dangerous in the 18th century, prompting local merchants to pay for construction of two wooden lighthouses at the northern tip of Plum Island in 1787. The lighthouses were ceded to the federal government in 1790 with the first keeper appointed by George Washington.

C. 1916

Lighthouse, Plum Island, Mass.

The original towers were built on moveable foundations so they could be easily relocated as the sandbars around Plum Island shifted. By lining up the two range lights mariners knew they were following the best channel into the harbor. In 1838 the lighthouses were replaced by a pair of octagonal towers, again on moveable foundations. A strange-looking small tower called the "Bug Light" was added in 1855; one of the lighthouses was destroyed by fire in 1856 but not rebuilt. The surviving lighthouse received a fourth-order Fresnel lens.

Shifting sands left the remaining tower and "Bug" too far inland, necessitating relocation several times between 1870 and 1898. Finally, in 1898, a new 45-foot wooden tower was built and the lens from the old light installed. The light was automated in 1951 and the Fresnel lens removed in 1981. The lighthouse now stands on the grounds of the Parker River National Wildlife Refuge headquarters; the tower is leased from the Coast Guard to the New England Lighthouse Foundation. Plans call for restoration of the tower's interior and conversion of the keeper's house into a museum.

Annisquam Light

The present Annisquam Light, also known as "Squam Light" and "Wigwam Light", is the third at this location. In 1801 the United States government bought the property from the Commonwealth of Massachusetts for $140.00. A wooden tower and wood-framed keeper's house were built; the house still stands with some modifications. The stone oil house built at that time also survives. By the 1820s the lighthouse was in poor condition, propped up with poles for a time. In 1851 a new octagonal, 40-foot wooden tower was built and a fifth-order Fresnel lens added in 1856.

A new 41-foot Federal-style brick tower was built in 1897 and in 1922 the kerosene-fueled light and fifth order lens were removed, replaced by an electrified fourth-order lens. The new light increased Annisquam Light's brightness from 1,300 to 250,000 candlepower. A fog signal was added in 1965; the lighthouse was automated in 1974.

Edward L. Hopper was born at this lighthouse in 1879, where his father was keeper from 1872-1894. In a letter he described a shipwreck which occurred around 1890. The *Abbie B. Cramer*, a three-masted

coal schooner from Baltimore, went ashore at the west end of Coffin's Beach, now called Wingaersheek Beach. All hands had to stay in the vessel's rigging awaiting help. Rescuers carried a lifeboat two miles across sand to reach the wreck and rescue the crew. Hopper claimed that years later he could see wood from the schooner protruding from the sand at low tide.

A Coast Guard family now lives at the light station. There is a small parking area, but the lighthouse is not open to the public.

Annisquam Harbor, circa 1904

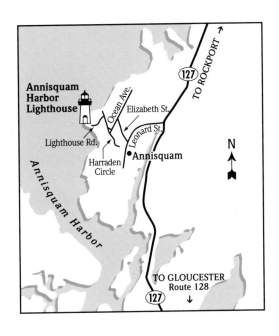

Directions:

From MA 127 (from Rockport or Gloucester) turn onto Leonard Rd.; this intersection is about 3 miles from the Grant Circle intersection of MA 128 and MA 127 and 1 mile from Plum Beach Cove Beach. At a "Norwood Heights" sign, turn right onto Elizabeth Rd. (about 0.3 mile). Cross Ocean Ave. to the intersection with Harraden Circle; turn right toward the harbor. Turn right, then left onto Lighthouse Rd. (0.7mile). The lighthouse is at the end of Lighthouse Rd. with a small parking area for "lighthouse viewing". Roads are not all marked.Tour boats out of Gloucester also offer good views.

Thacher Island Lights
(Thatchers, Cape Ann)

Thachers Island, off Rockport on Cape Ann, was named by Anthony Thacher, an Englishman whose fishing vessel, the *Watch and Wait*, was wrecked near the island in 1635. Thacher and his wife, Elizabeth, were the only survivors of the wreck in which 21 people died; Thacher was awarded the island to recompense him for his losses.

In 1771 there were only three lighthouses in operation north of Cape Cod: Boston, Plymouth and Portsmouth. To this point, lighthouses were built to mark port entrances; the construction of twin towers on Thachers Island in 1771 marked the first such lights to mark a "dangerous spot." Two 45-foot stone towers, about 300 yards apart, were lighted for the first time on December 21, 1771; the station was ceded to the federal government in 1790.

The lights at Thacher Island were the first seen by many coming from Europe into Massachusetts Bay. In 1810 the south tower became the second lighthouse (after Boston) to receive a new Argand lamp and parabolic reflector. A new stone house was built in 1816 (it still stands) and a fog bell installed in 1853. New, taller (124 foot) towers were built in 1861 and Fresnel lenses installed.

South Light

On December 21, 1864 keeper Alexander Bray left for the mainland to take an ailing assistant keeper to the doctor. His wife, Maria, and 14-year-old nephew Sidney Haskell were left at the light station. Later that day a heavy snow storm swept the area, making it impossible for Bray to return to the island. For two nights Maria Bray and Sidney Haskell braved high winds and heavy snow to light the lamps in both towers; each tower had 148 steps with three trips needed to keep the lamps filled with oil and lantern room panes free of soot.

North Light

"Thacher Island Twin Lights
Rockport, Massachusetts
has been placed on the National Register
of Historic Places by the
United States Department of the Interior
October 7, 1971"

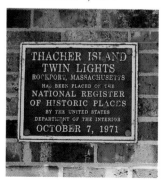

North Light

South Light

18

South Light

Despite the twin lights, many wrecks still occurred in the vicinity. In November 1898 a ferocious storm struck the New England coast. The most famous casualty of the storm was the steamer *Portland*, lost with 200 people on board.

In 1932 the north light was extinguished and the south light intensified to 70,000 candlepower. The south light and fog signal were automated in 1980. Concerned citizens of Cape Ann formed the Thachers Island Association and chose a caretaker to live on the island. In 1989 the north light was restored and opened to visitors. There are no longer caretakers on the island; the boat ramp was washed away in the winter of 1995 making landing impossible. Views are possible from shore or from tour boats.

South Light

Directions:

The twin lighthouses are visible in the distance from along MA 127A. For clearer views, turn east at the South Street-Thatcher Rd. signs (1.5 miles north of the "Entering Rockport" sign or 1.2 miles south of Marmion Way in Rockport). There is a "triangle" at the intersection. At Penzance Rd. turn left and continue to Old Penzance Rd. Turn left onto Old Penzance Rd. which becomes a dirt road. There is an open field for parking at the road's end. A good view of the lighthouses is possible from the rocky knoll known as Loblolly Knoll. For a time the Thachers Island Association offered trips to the island. However landing is now impossible after a 1995 storm washed out the boat ramp. The lighthouses are best photographed by boat.

Straitsmouth Island Light

Rockport's vital granite business began in the 1820s and, together with the already flourishing fishing industry, put the town on the map. Straitsmouth Island light was built in 1835 to assist mariners with entry into the harbor at nearby Pigeon Cove. Several vessels were lost in storms in the 1830s and 1840s in the vicinity of the island, prompting placement of a warning buoy near Avery's Rock nearby.

In the 1850s a new Fresnel lens was installed and in 1896 the present 37-foot brick tower built to replace the old one. The light was converted from white to green in 1932, automated in 1967 and the Fresnel lens subsequently removed. The island was sold to private ownership in 1941, but was eventually acquired by the Massachusetts Audubon Society; the property is now part of the Ipswich Wildlife Sanctuary.

The 1835 wooden keeper's house still stands but is currently boarded up and in disrepair. Although the old entryway to the tower was destroyed by a storm in October, 1991, it has since been replaced; an oil house also remains.The lighthouse can be seen in the distance from the breakwater at the end of Bearskin Neck in Rockport or from some of the excursion cruises in the area.

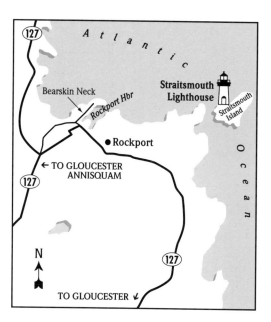

Directions:

The lighthouse is located at the entrance to Rockport Harbor and can be seen at a distance from the end of Bearskin Neck (pedestrian area which ends at the breakwater). Rockport is reached from MA 127/127A from North or South; it is a congested area with limited parking near the waterfront. The wharf is the site of the much-photographed and painted Motif #1 (harbor, lobster boats). The lighthouse is best photographed by boat.

Ten Pound Island Light

Ten Pound Island, in Gloucester harbor, achieved notoriety in 1817 when several people reported seeing a large sea serpent on the ledges on the island's eastern side. Among the witnesses was Amos Story. In 1821 a 40-foot stone lighthouse, keeper's house and oil house were built and Mr. Story, the sea serpent descriptor, became the first keeper in 1833. A new 30-foot cast-iron tower, lined with brick, was built in 1881.

Over the years, the island has hosted a fish hatchery, artist Winslow Homer and a Coast Guard air station intended to catch rum runners during prohibition. In 1956 Ten Pound Island light was decommissioned and the fifth-order Fresnel lens removed; the new optic was put on the old bell tower, then later moved to a skeleton tower. The house and outbuildings had been reduced to rubble. Ownership of the island reverted to the town of Gloucester.

The Lighthouse Preservation Society initiated restoration of the lighthouse in the 1980s, with federal and private funds obtained. The tower was repaired and the automatic light returned. Ten Pound Island light was relighted as an active aid to navigation on August 7, 1989; the oil house was restored in 1995. The light can be seen from many points along the Gloucester waterfront or from tour boats.

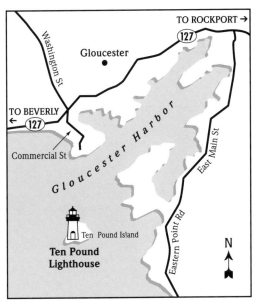

Directions:

The light can be seen from Pavilion Beach Park on MA 127 (Main St.) about 1 mile west of the Washington and Commercial intersection and just east of the draw bridge in Gloucester. A small beach area immediately outside the entrance to the Eastern Point area also offers distant views. Excursion boat trips from Gloucester offer the best views and pass by several other lighthouses as well.

Eastern Point Light

The first stone lighthouse tower at Eastern Point, completed in 1832, was intended to aid fishermen and mariners entering Gloucester Harbor. This light assumed new importance with the arrival of the railroad and subsequent increase in fishing business. A new 34-foot lighthouse was built in 1848; its revolving light was turned by a clockwork mechanism wound periodically by the keeper. A fog bell also was operated by similar mechanism.

The present (third) Eastern Point Light was built in 1890 on the old foundation of the 1832 tower. The 36-foot brick lighthouse, attached to the keeper's house by covered walkway, received a fourth-order Fresnel lens. This lens was removed in 1919 and replaced by a rotating aero-beacon. The two-story duplex house that still stands was built in 1879; the oil house survives from 1894. The garage and fog signal are more recent, built in 1947 and 1951 respectively. At the end of the 2,250-foot breakwater there is a strictly utilitarian light, marking the dangerous Dog Bar Reef. Both lights were automated in 1986.

The Coast Guard made repairs to the station in 1993 and a Coast Guard family now lives in the keeper's house.

There is a parking area at the station but the grounds are closed to the public. You can walk along the breakwater for excellent views of the lighthouse. Tour boats from Gloucester also pass the light.

Gloucester Breakwater light

C. 1907

Directions:

From Rt 128 in Gloucester follow East Main St. to Niles Beach and the entrance to Eastern Point at Eastern Point Boulevard West. This road leads through an exclusive residential area marked with "Residents Only" and "Private" signs. The road is a public right-of-way and visitors are allowed to drive directly to the lighthouse. There is a parking area at the lighthouse with good views from that area and along the granite breakwater. The tour boats out of Gloucester also offer good photo opportunities.

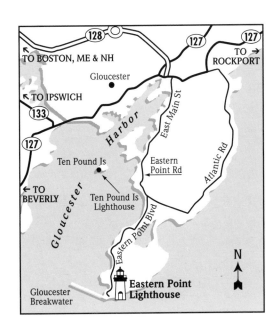

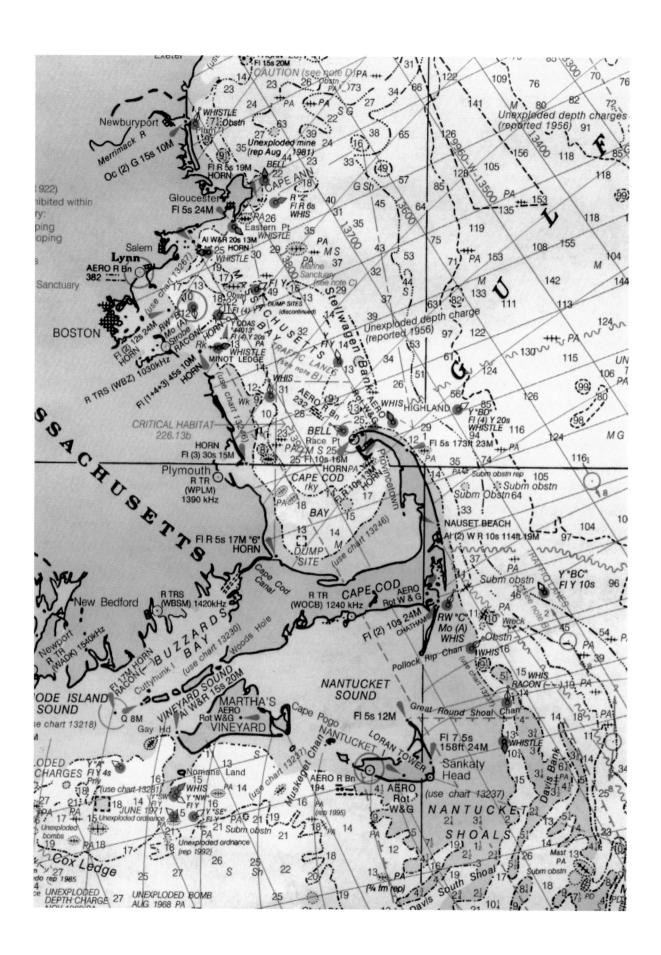

Salem Harbor & Shore

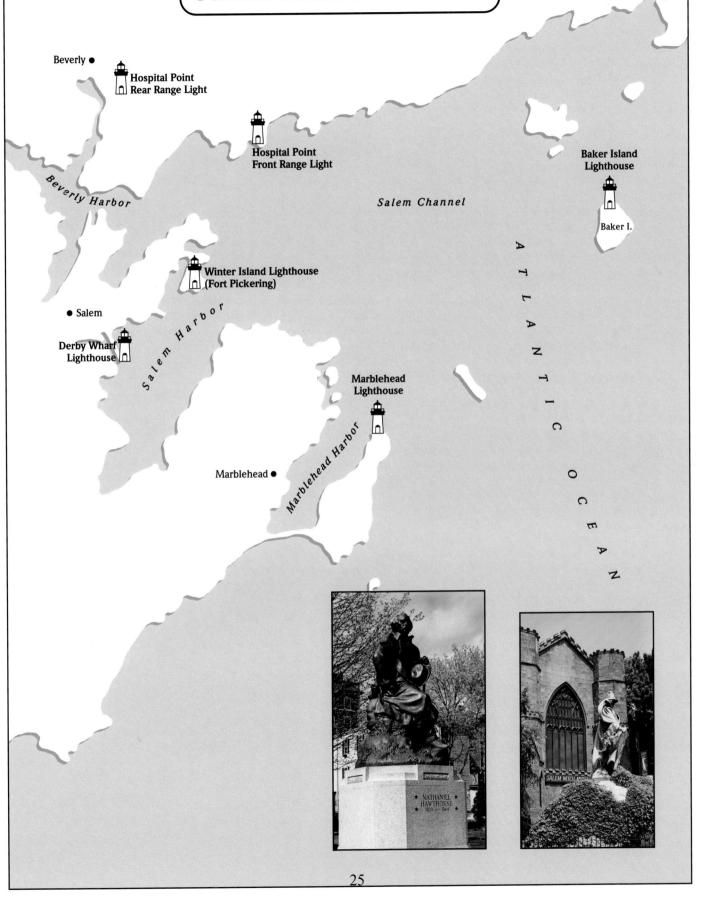

Beverly ●

Hospital Point
Rear Range Light

Hospital Point
Front Range Light

Beverly Harbor

Salem Channel

Baker Island
Lighthouse

Baker I.

Winter Island Lighthouse
(Fort Pickering)

● Salem

Derby Wharf
Lighthouse

Salem Harbor

Marblehead
Lighthouse

Marblehead ●

Marblehead Harbor

A T L A N T I C   O C E A N

Bakers Island Light

At the entrance to Salem Harbor, Bakers Island was first annexed to Salem in 1630 and has long been home to summer residents. In 1791, a day marker was placed on the island. Because this was inadequate for the increased shipping traffic in the area, Congress authorized the construction of twin lighthouses on Bakers Island. The first Bakers Island lights were lit on January 3, 1798 with the two towers located atop the keeper's house, at either end of the building.

For a time one of Bakers Island's twin lights was extinguished. Mariners claimed this made it difficult to distinguish this light from Boston Light and an increased number of wrecks attested to the confusion. New towers were subsequently built and lighted in 1821. One of the towers was slightly taller than the other leading to the nickname "Mr. & Mrs. Lighthouses". The taller light received a fourth-order Fresnel lens in 1855.

When, in 1907, a new air siren replaced the old fog bell at the lighthouse, complaints of the island residents were vehement. The signal was then redirected toward the sea through a megaphone so that it was barely audible on the island.

In 1916 the smaller lighthouse was discontinued and subsequently torn down. At that time the taller tower received an acetylene-powered lamp;it now houses a modern plastic optic.The light was automated in 1972.

In 1887 Dr. Nathan Morse of Salem bought the entire island, except the lighthouse and station. He built a large health spa, the Winne-egan and proclaimed the Bakers Island air "highly charged with ozone from the ocean". Former President Benjamin Harrison and Actress Lillian Russell were among visitors to Bakers Island in the Winne-egan heyday.

The spa burned in 1906. Bakers Island still has a sizable summer colony, despite tales of ghostly hauntings. Today, the island is managed by the Bakers Island Association, founded in 1914.

Baker's Island Light, Salem, Mass.

C- 1907

Directions:

From MA 127 in Manchester-by-the-Sea, turn east onto Harbor Street (about .6 miles from Highland Ave., 0.5 miles from Pine St.). Bear right as the road narrows into an exclusive residential area. The view of the lighthouse from the beach is distant and binoculars are required. The best views are obtained by boat; excursion trips run by Boston Harbor Explorers, Friends of Boston Harbor Islands and others pass this light.

27

Hospital Point Range Lights

Like neighboring Salem, Beverly was an active port for both trade and fishing in the 18th and 19th centuries. Hospital Point, Derby Wharf and Fort Pickering Lighthouses all were built in 1871 to guide vessels into the harbors. The 45-foot Federal-style lighthouse is located at the former site of a smallpox hospital, the area having become known as "hospital point".The two-story keeper's house still stands, with major additions in 1968 almost surrounding the actual lighthouse. The original oil house also remains.

Hospital Point light still has the original 3 1/2- order Fresnel lens with condensing panel in front. This panel, considered unique to American lighthouses, causes the light intensity to diminish as the mariner veers from the main channel into Salem Harbor.

In 1927 the light officially became Hospital Point Range Front Light; a rear range light was placed in the steeple of the First Baptist Church one mile away. The steeple light is aligned with the front range light to further guide vessels into Salem Harbor.Automated in 1947, this lighthouse has since been home to the Commander of the First Coast Guard District. The lighthouse is easily accessible but grounds are not opened. At dead low tide walking from nearby Ober Street Beach takes you in front of the lighthouse.

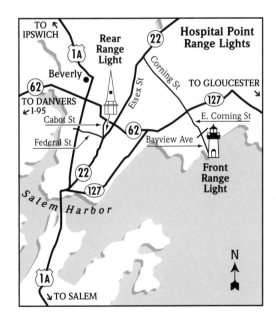

Directions:

In Beverly, turn east from MA 127 onto East Corning Street (approximately 0.4 miles northeast of the MA 62 and MA 127 junction). Bear left at Bayview Ave. and continue to the road's end in a cul-de-sac and the front range light. At low tide it is possible to walk around the beach from Lynch Park to get a front view of the light. At the intersection of Neptune/Ober St. and East Corning, turn right and continue bearing right to Ober St. The park is to the left. The rear range light is located in steeple of the First Baptist Church located at the intersection of Cabot, Federal and Dane Streets.

Winter Island (Fort Pickering) Light

Winter Island light, also known as Fort Pickering Light, was built in 1871, along with Derby Wharf and Hospital Point lights. With the addition of these new lights, mariners would line up Winter Island and Derby Wharf lights after passing Bakers Island on the way into Salem harbor. The lighthouse was built of iron lined with brick and exhibited a flashing white light 28 feet above sea level.

The island was the site of 18th century Fort Pickering, much of which still stands; several 19th century hangings were held at the island's Gallows Hill and the grounds served as a militia training ground.

A Coast Guard airplane hanger was located on Winter Island in 1934 with Coast Guard personnel living in the old keeper's house while new quarters were built. The keeper's house and outbuildings were later removed.

The lighthouse was deactivated in 1969 and fell into disrepair. A group of concerned citizens saved the lighthouse and it was relighted in 1983 as a private aid to navigation, then converted to solar power in 1994.

Winter Island Lighthouse, Salem Willows, Mass.

Fort Pickering, Winter Island

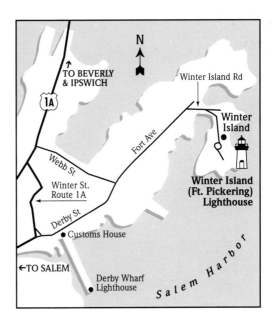

Directions:

Take MA 1A into Salem; turn left (south) at Webb St. Bear left (east) at Fort Avenue, then right at Winter Island Road ("Winter Island Marine Recreation Area" sign). From Salem, follow 1A to Derby Street/Fort Avenue then continue to Winter Island Road and the entrance to the park. There are a variety of ways to enter the Salem area; directional signs to Winter Island are posted frequently to guide you.

31

Derby Wharf Light

For many years the twin lights at Bakers Island had sufficed to guide vessels into Salem Harbor, but it was decided another light was needed to help mariners find their way into the crowded inner harbor. The unusual 12-foot square, 25-foot tall brick lighthouse was built and put into service in 1871. Because of proximity to the city, Derby Wharf light always had a caretaker rather than resident keeper.

The original fifth-order Fresnel was changed in 1906 to a fourth-order with flashing red light. In 1910 reclassification to a harbor light required replacement with a sixth-order lens (reverting to fixed light). The light was automated in the 1970s, then deactivated in 1977 with ownership going to the National Park Service. In 1983 the Friends of Salem Maritime had Derby Wharf relighted as a private aid to navigation with solar-powered optic. The wharf dates back to the 1760s and is part of the Salem National Historic Park. The Customs House where Nathaniel Hawthorne worked is across the street and the House of Seven Gables nearby.

Custom House opposite Derby Wharf

32

Looking back from the wharf

Salem Common

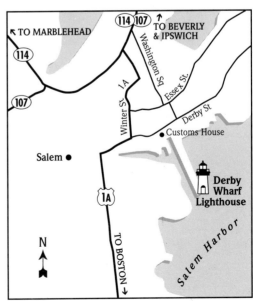

Directions:

Follow MA 1A, 114 or 107 into Salem. Turn east onto
Derby Street (Derby St. is also reached by following
Washington Square east from MA 1A or Fort Avenue
from Winter Island). The lighthouse is at the end of the
wharf opposite the restored Customs House and about
three blocks from the House of Seven Gables.

Marblehead Light

Over the years many have noted how much more scenic the picturesque harbor would be if Marblehead Light was a traditional white lighthouse instead of a metal skeleton tower. Edward Rowe Snow wrote "..it is to be realized that lighthouses are for utility and not for beauty, but in this case it is especially unfortunate that beauty and utility were not combined."

The first lighthouse in the part of Marblehead Neck known as Point O'Neck was of the traditional style: white tower attached to keeper's house with covered walkway. However, with the growing popularity of Marblehead Neck as a summer resort, large "cottages" sprung up around the lighthouse, obscuring it from view from the sea.

Point Light, Marblehead Neck, Mass.

The present structure, built in 1895, was intended to ensure visibility. Composed of eight cast-iron pilings connected by supports, the tower includes a spiral stairway with 105 steps leading to the lantern room.

"Marblehead Light
Est. 1882...By permission of congress..Original stone lighthouse was replaced by present structure of iron in 1888...130 ft above sea level...visibility app. 20 miles..First keeper of the light was Ezekiel Darling, a gunner in the old frigate constelation.."

34

The keeper's house is gone, but a brick oil house still stands. Past requests from town officials to paint the structure white obviously have been unsuccessful as the tower remains a "military brown."

The light was originally fitted with a Fresnel lens, exhibiting a steady white light; this characteristic was later changed to red, then green making Marblehead the only such light on the coast. The light was automated in 1960 and a plastic optic installed. Lighthouse grounds are now a park area.

Directions:

Follow MA 114 into Marblehead from Salem or MA 129 from Lynn. Turn east onto Ocean Avenue and cross a causeway, bearing left into Harbor Avenue. Reconnect with Ocean Avenue at follow it to its end at Follett Street (one way). Continue into Chandler Hovey Park. The light tower can also be seen at a distance from Front Street in Marblehead by following MA 114 to its end and continuing to the town wharf.

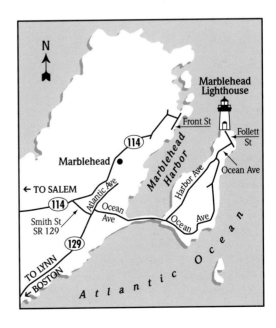

Boston Harbor

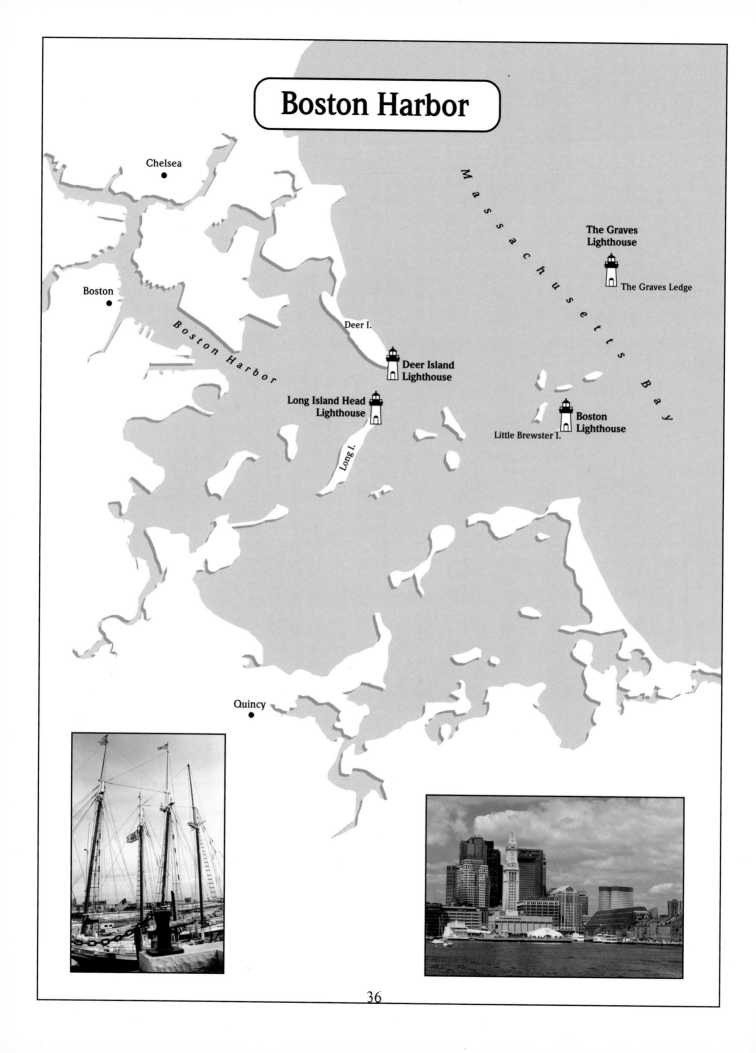

Chelsea

Boston

Deer I.

Boston Harbor

Deer Island
Lighthouse

Long Island Head
Lighthouse

Long I.

Massachusetts Bay

The Graves
Lighthouse

The Graves Ledge

Boston
Lighthouse

Little Brewster I.

Quincy

Boston Light

Called the "ideal American lighthouse" by historian Edward Rowe Snow, Boston light holds an honored place among lighthouses. It was the first lighthouse built in North America and is the only one in the United States today which has not been automated. Because the lighthouse was destroyed in the Revolution and rebuilt in 1783, the tower itself is the nation's second oldest.

Because Boston was the maritime center of colonial America, there were lighted beacons in the area before Boston light, but these were only lanterns on poles. In 1713 a Boston merchant representing the city's business community proposed a lighthouse to mark the entrance to the harbor; on July 23, 1715 the Boston Light Bill was passed. A stone tower was then built on Little Brewster Island, financed by a one-cent-per-ton tax on all vessels entering or leaving the harbor. The light was placed in service September 14, 1716 by the first keeper, George Worthylake. Several fires did substantial damage to the lighthouse tower during the 18th century, some apparently caused by lightening. However, a lightening rod was never put on the tower as it was thought that such a device would go against the will of God.

Photo by John Forbes

37

In July 1775, with Boston Harbor under British control, American troops were sent to the island where they burned parts of the tower. The British immediately began repairing the lighthouse, but American soldiers again landed and were easy victors over the British guard; the lighthouse was again burned. At the close of the Revolution the British lingered in Boston harbor for some months. When leaving the area in June of 1776, troops set off a timed charge on Little Brewster Island, completely destroying the lighthouse. The remains of the metal lantern were used to make ladles for American cannons.

Reconstruction of Boston light wasn't completed until 1783. The new 75-foot tall rubblestone tower was built on order of John Hancock, then governor of Massachusetts, and became property of the federal government in1789. In 1859 the light was raised to its present height of 89 feet.A new lantern room was added to house a 12-sided, second-order Fresnel lens which revolved on machinery run by a clockwork mechanism. A keeper's duplex was also built during that year, then a second keeper's house added in 1885 to accommodate the three keepers assigned to the light. In the 1930s 16 children among the three keepers' families were at home on one-acre Little Brewster Island.

Boston Light

The Coast Guard took over operation of Boston light in 1941. During World War II the light was extinguished, then brought back into operation in July 1945. The light was electrified in 1948 and an electric motor replaced the clockwork mechanism that rotated the lens; the original Fresnel lens remains in place, visible for 27 miles. In 1960 the duplex keepers' house was burned.

Coast Guard staff now alternate two-week duty rotations on the island, often accompanied by an animal companion. A mutt named Farah lived on Little Brewster for 13 years and a recent frisky black feline resident was named Ida Lewis, after America's most famous woman lighthouse keeper. The gravestone of Farah, "beloved mutt" can be seen near the lighthouse. Odd happenings also have been reported at the station: a radio mysteriously changing channels from rock to classical and the figure of a man sitting in the lantern room seen by a recent keeper when he and his assistant were the only ones on the island.

Boston light was named a National Historic Landmark in 1964, one of three lighthouses to receive this designation. The light was scheduled for automation in 1989, completing the process of automating all United States lighthouses. Preservation groups appealed and funding was appropriated to keep Coast Guard staff on the island, operating the light and other equipment as a living museum of lighthouse history. Meteorological data and daily positions of 25 navigational aids are recorded.

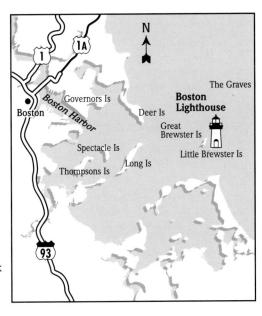

Directions:
Friends of Boston Harbor Islands and the Boston Harbor Explorers schedule excursions which offer close views of the light and, in some cases, landing on the island for a brief visit. **Friends of Boston Harbor Island Boat Trips, 349 Lincoln St.- Bldg 45, Hingham, MA 02114 (617) 740-4290. Boston Harbor Explorers P.O. Box 744, Quincy, MA. 02269 (617) 479-1871**

Boston Light

Recent storms have done serious damage to the island and, despite erosion control measures, Boston light will eventually be threatened by the sea. In 1990 a Stewardship Plan and preservation guidelines for the island and light were commissioned. As a result of that study, much recent work has been done on the island, including the keeper's house and outbuildings. Friends of Boston Harbor Islands offers trips to Little Brewster Island each summer; names of visitors dating back to the 18th century can be seen carved into the rocks and the view of Boston harbor is breathtaking.

Deer Island Light

No more than a light on a fiberglass pole, the present Deer Island Light is built strictly with utility in mind. The light is located south of the Town of Winthrop, about 500 yards from Deer Island. The island itself has an unpleasant past as an internment camp for Indians, site of a state prison and immigrant quarantine station; a sewage treatment plant is now on the island.

The first Deer Island light was a sparkplug-type, built in 1890 to mark a treacherous sandbar and to indicate the ship channel along President Roads into Boston Harbor. Painted brown, the old lighthouse has been described as a three-tier wedding cake with chocolate frosting.

Several particularly notable tales are associated with this light. The most tragic incident took place in 1916. The keeper, Joseph McCabe, left the lighthouse to meet his fiancee on Deer Island to address wedding invitations. Ice around the lighthouse trapped McCabe's boat, so he decided to walk across the sandbar. Nearing the island, he lost his footing and disappeared into the ocean, drowning in the icy waves. Tom Small became keeper in 1931, bringing with him a cat that gained fame as the "climbing cat of Deer Island Light." Reportedly, Small's cat would leap into the water, emerge with a fish, climb the ladder and eat the catch. Finally, it seems that during the days of prohibition, the keepers were illegally brewing malt liquor at the lighthouse. When an inspector arrived without notice the enterprise was abruptly put to rest.

By the early 1980s Deer Island light had deteriorated to the point of being unsafe. In 1982, much to the surprise and dismay of area residents, the iron lighthouse was removed and replaced by a 51-foot fiberglass, matchstick-like modular tower set on the original caisson.

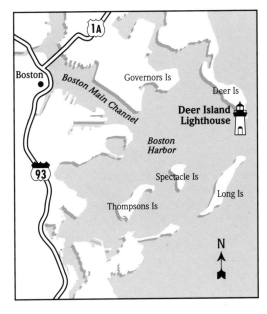

Directions: Excursion boats from Boston will pass this light, although at varying distances; trips with Friends of Boston Harbor Islands or Boston Harbor Explorers are examples. The light can also be seen at a distance from the shore on Winthrop Beach in Winthrop, MA.

41

Graves Light

A new major shipping channel into Boston Harbor (Broad Sound Channel), which opened in the early 20th century, necessitated the building of a lighthouse at the ledges called the Graves. The ledges were named in the 1600s for Thomas Graves, Vice-Admiral of Governor Winthrop's Navy.

The building of the 113-foot Graves light took place from 1903 to 1905. Granite for the light was cut at Rockport, MA.. Rock on the ledges was blasted and the foundation laid just four feet above the low tide mark. When it went into service, the Graves Light was measured at 380,000 candlepower with a first-order Fresnel lens. The light was later upgraded to 3.2 million candlepower, and for many years was the most powerful along the New England coast.

The keepers lived in the third, fourth and fifth stories, with the entrance to the lighthouse at the top of a 40-foot ladder. A water cistern was filled twice each year by a lighthouse tender; in addition to regular food deliveries, keepers augmented their diet with lobsters from traps they tended around the ledges.

Noted among the several wrecks in the vicinity of Graves Light was the *City of Salisbury* in 1938, remembered as the "Zoo Ship" for its cargo of zoo animals. The ship struck a reef close to the Graves, but no lives were lost and she became a tourist attraction for a few months before splitting in two and sinking.

Storms have destroyed the walkway and vandals have caused thousands of dollars in damage to the lighthouse; the fog signal was swept away by the "No-Name Storm" of October, 1991. The landing platform was repaired in 1993 and the original oil house still stands. The Graves Light was automated in 1976. Its Fresnel lens, 12 feet high and nine feet in diameter, is in storage at the Smithsonian Institution.

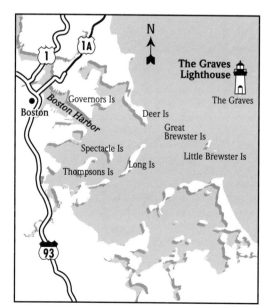

The light is best viewed by boat; Friends of Boston Habor Islands and Harbor Explorers both offer trips which pass this lighthouse.

Long Island Head Light

The longest island in Boston Harbor, Long Island has been home to a resort hotel, military fortifications and a hospital. Legend has it that the island is haunted by the "Woman in Scarlet", the ghost of the wife of a British solider killed by cannon fire in 1776 and buried on the island.

In 1819 the first stone lighthouse tower was built on a hill on Long Island Head to guide vessels entering the harbor. The site is second only to Boston Light as the harbor's oldest light station, sometimes referred to as Inner Harbor Light. A 3-1/2

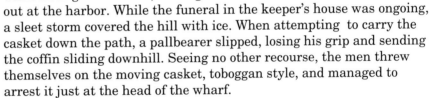

order Fresnel lens was installed in the 1850s. A new 52-foot brick lighthouse was constructed about 1900 to make room for enlargement of the island's fortification, Fort Strong. This was the third lighthouse on Long Island Head; construction date of the second tower is uncertain.

The last keeper, Edwin Tarr, died while sitting in his chair, looking out at the harbor. While the funeral in the keeper's house was ongoing, a sleet storm covered the hill with ice. When attempting to carry the casket down the path, a pallbearer slipped, losing his grip and sending the coffin sliding downhill. Seeing no other recourse, the men threw themselves on the moving casket, toboggan style, and managed to arrest it just at the head of the wharf.

After being discontinued in 1982, a solar-powered optic was installed, the tower renovated and the light reactivated in 1985. The keeper's house and outbuildings no longer remain. Although there is a bridge to the island to provide access to other buildings, entrance is closely guarded and visiting the lighthouse not permitted. A variety of boats out of Boston Harbor pass this lighthouse.

Directions:

All boats from Long Wharf to George's Island pass Long Island Head; there are 5-6 departures daily during summer months. Any excursion boat from Rowe's or Long Wharf will pass this light, although the views vary in distance.

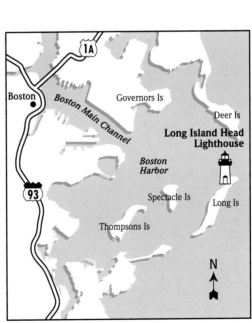

43

The South Shore

Boston ●

Boston Harbor

A T L A N T I C O C E A N

Minots Ledge Lighthouse

Quincy ●

Scituate Lighthouse

Scituate ●

Duxbury ●

Plymouth Lighthouse (The Gurnet)

Duxbury Pier Lighthouse

Plymouth ●

Duxbury Pier Light

Built in 1871 on the north side of the main channel in Plymouth Harbor, this lighthouse marks the dangerous shoal off Saquish Head. The unusual coffeepot-shaped lighthouse is known locally as "Bug Light" or "The Bug". There are three levels which were used as living quarters; the lantern room held a fourth-order Fresnel lens.

The light was automated in 1965 and during the next two decades fell victim to vandalism. In 1983, with Duxbury Pier light slated for replacement with a tower similar to that of Deer Island, a group of local residents formed Project Bug Light. The group convinced the Coast Guard to alter those plans and a five-year lease was granted to the preservation committee. The Coast Guard refurbished the lower half of the lighthouse while the Project Bug group raised funds to restore the interior and upper parts. Solar power replaced the battery system.

However, the Project Bug Light dissolved after a few years, the five-year lease expired and plans were again made to replace the lighthouse. A new preservation effort was undertaken and the Coast Guard again refurbished the lighthouse in 1996; fund raising for maintenance is ongoing. Although the light can be seen distantly from the Plymouth waterfront, best views are from the harbor cruises and whale watches out of Plymouth.

DUXBURY PIER LIGHT, PLYMOUTH HARBOR, MASS.

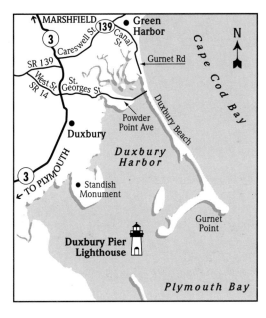

Directions:

From the intersection of RTs 14 and 139, bear right (east) and continue on RT 14 (West St.). Cross MA 3 and continue straight as the road becomes St. Georges St. Follow this road to Powder Point Ave. which ends at a bridge to the Gurnet peninsula and beach parking area. The light may be seen from Duxbury Beach and the Gurnet peninsula; a four-wheel drive vehicle is required to drive past the parking areas onto the Gurnet. Additionally, the light may be viewed at a distance from Plymouth Harbor or more closely from excursion boats from the Plymouth Municipal Pier.

Minots Ledge Light

In 1847, lighthouse inspector I.W.P. Lewis compiled a report on dangerous Minots Ledge off Boston's south shore. The report noted that more than 40 vessels had been lost on the ledge from 1832 to 1841, with property damage in excess of $360,000. Lewis stated that need for a lighthouse at Minots Ledge was greater than anywhere else in New England.

This recommendation led to construction of the first lighthouse at the ledge built between 1847 and 1850, lighted for the first time January 1, 1850. Minots was the first lighthouse in the United States to be exposed to the ocean's full fury and the first two keepers deemed the structure unsafe. These fears proved well founded. In April of 1851 a storm struck the New England coast, flooding Boston and much of the area. People on shore the night of April 16 heard the fog bell at the lighthouse, then sudden silence. Two assistant keepers were killed and legend tells that, in dark and stormy weather, a voice can be heard coming from Minots light warning, "Stay Away!"

From 1851 to 1860 a lightship replaced the tower and work on a new stone tower was undertaken in 1855.

This structure has been called the greatest achievement in American lighthouse engineering. Because construction could take place only at low tide on calm days, the cutting and assembling of the granite took place on Government Island. A total of 1,079 blocks of Quincy granite were placed.

C- 1850

"So it may stand, that 'they who go down to the sea in ships' may see this signal fire burning brightly to warn them from the countless rocks that echo with the rage that oft swells from the bosom of old ocean."

Cap't. Barton Alexander,
Superintendant of Minots Light construction

Many times during the construction waves swept workers off the rocks but the project continued and the last stone was placed at Minots Ledge on June 29, 1860. The lantern room and second-order Fresnel lens were installed and the lighthouse illuminated on August 22, 1860. Although waves have been known to sweep over the top of the lighthouse, the structure has withstood countless storms and hurricanes, a testament to the designers and builders.

A well in the lower part of the tower, filled twice yearly, held the water supply for the keepers. A member of a group of young ladies touring the lighthouse asked the keeper about the well. He answered,"That's our bathtub. It goes down 40 feet." Mulling this over, the lady replied, " You must be out of luck when you drop the soap." In 1893 Minots was given a new optic and a distinctive characteristic 1-4-3 flash. Someone allowed that 1-4-3 stood for "I Love You", giving rise to the nickname the "I Love You Light".

The lighthouse was automated in 1947 and the Fresnel lens replaced; in 1983 the light was converted to solar power. In 1992-93 the keeper's house at Government Island was restored with funds raised by the Cohasset Lightkeepers Corporation. At Government Island, a replica of the lantern room of Minots light sits atop some of the granite blocks removed from the lighthouse during a renovation in 1989; the fog bell also is on display.

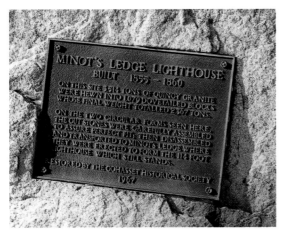

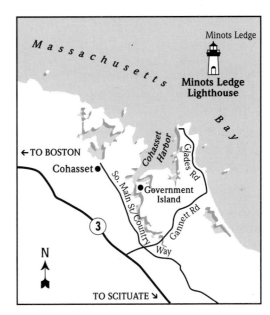

Directions:

The land views of the lighthouse are distant from Sandy Beach in Cohasset. From Cohasset center, turn east on Highland Ave then east onto Beach St. Continue to Atlantic Ave. and turn left; the beach is about 0.5 mile north. Minots is best photographed from the water; excursion boats out of Boston Harbor which specifically offer "lighthouse trips" (Friends of Boston Harbor Is. or Harbor Explorers) usually try to get to this lighthouse. However, sea conditions are often unpredictable in the area making close views of the light impossible.

Scituate Light

By the late 18th century Scituate had become a major fishing port, due in large part to its protected harbor. However, shallow water and mudflats made entering the harbor difficult and, in 1810, pressure from town officials convinced the federal government to appropriate $4000 for construction of a lighthouse at the harbor entrance. Completed in 1811, the 25-foot stone tower exhibited a white light 30 feet above sea level and was accompanied by a keeper's house, oil vault and well.

The first keeper of Scituate Light was Simeon Bates who remained at the lighthouse until his death in 1834. Bates and his wife, Rachel, had nine children, including teenage daughters Rebecca and Abigail. During the War of 1812, British warships frequently raided New England coastal towns, including Scituate.In September 1814, such a raid was attempted as a warship anchored close to the Scituate lighthouse.

The only members of the Bates family at the station were Rebecca and Abigail. The sisters, seeing a party of British soldiers rowing toward shore, realized there wasn't time to warn

others. They grabbed their fife and drum and played loudly; the unsuspecting British thought the Scituate town militia was approaching and hastily retreated. Thus was created the legend of Scituate's "Light-

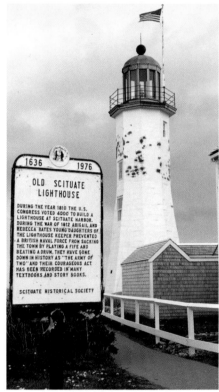

house Army of Two." Some have claimed the ghosts of Rebecca and Abigail Bates haunt Scituate Light. Fife and drum music, they say, can be heard blending in with wind and waves.

48

In 1827 a 15-foot brick extension and new lantern room were added to the lighthouse to increase its visibility. A white-over-red configuration (white top light, red light in lower windows) was intended to allow mariners to differentiate between Scituate and Boston lights. However, the white and red lights tended to merge from a distance and vessels continued to crash into the dangerous offshore ledges.

The lighthouse gradually deteriorated and the completion of Minots Light in 1850 signalled the end for Scituate light. When the first Minots light was destroyed in a storm in 1852, Scituate light went back into service and it received a new Fresnel lens in 1855. In 1860 the second Minots was lighted and Scituate extinguished.

In 1916 the U.S. Lighthouse Establishment put Scituate Light up for sale. A hastily organized deposit of $1000 secured the property for the Town of Scituate. Among those who later contributed to the $4000 purchase price was a grand nephew of Abigail and Rebecca Bates.

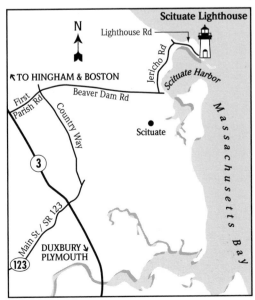

The town made some initial improvements and did major work on the keeper's house in the 1960s. In 1988 the light was placed on the National Register of Historic Places and in 1994 was relighted as a private aid to navigation. Today contributions and rent from residents of the keeper's house pay for upkeep of the property.

Directions:
From MA 3, take the MA 123 exit east to MA 3A .Bear left onto Country Way and continue to the intersection with First Parish Rd. Or, coming from the north on MA 3A, turn left onto First Parish Rd. **Both** MA 3A and Country Way intersect with First Parish Rd. Bear right onto Beaver Dam Rd. (First Parish bears left), continue to the intersection with Jericho Rd. and turn left. Continue to Lighthouse Rd.; bear right to the lighthouse. There is a parking area.

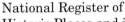

Plymouth Light

The area around Plymouth and the Gurnet was visited and mapped by explorer Samuel de Champlain in 1606. The name apparently referred to similar areas in England which were named after the abundant fish called gurnet. Plymouth became a major port of colonial America and shipping traffic necessitated a navigational aid at the entrance to the harbor. In 1769 the first lighthouse was erected on the high bluff at the end of the long Gurnet peninsula; the house, with two lantern rooms on the roof, was the first site of "twin lights" in North America.

The original lighthouse was built on the land of John and Hannah Thomas; he would serve as the first keeper and, after his death, she became America's first woman lightkeeper. This twin structure served until 1801 when it was destroyed by an oil fire; new twin towers were built in 1803, 30 feet apart. However, there were complaints that the Gurnet's two lights blended into one from a distance and were easily confused with Barnstable's Sandy Neck Light. In 1843 the towers were replaced with octagonal wooden structures, 34 feet high and connected with a covered walkway. The problem of "merging lights" remained and in 1871 the power of the lights was increased by installation of fourth-order Fresnel lenses.

Gurnet Lights and Keeper's Residence, Plymouth, Mass.

Gurnet Light, Plymouth, Mass.

The importance of Plymouth light gradually decreased as commerce declined. In 1924 the northeast light was discontinued; the foundation is still visible next to the remaining structure. The light was automated in 1986 and converted to solar power in 1994; a modern optic replaced the Fresnel lens. The Massachusetts chapter of the U.S. Lighthouse Society was granted lease to the lighthouse in the late 1980s but the lease has since reverted to the Coast Guard. The lighthouse was moved back from the eroding cliff in the fall of 1997.

Directions:
From RT 3, take the RT 14/Duxbury exit east. Bear left at the intersection with MA 139 (Careswell St.) and continue to Canal St. Turning right follow Canal St.; the road becomes Gurnet Rd. and ends at parking areas for Duxbury Beach. A four-wheel drive vehicle is required for the remainder of the drive along the sandy peninsula to its end at the lighthouse. A permit also may be needed.

Or.. From the intersection of RTs 14 and 139, bear right and continue on RT 14 (West St.). Cross MA 3 and continue straight as the road becomes St. Georges St. Follow this road to Powder Point Ave. which ends at a bridge to the Gurnet peninsula and beach parking area.

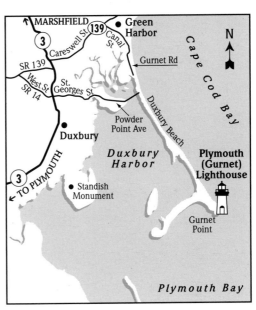

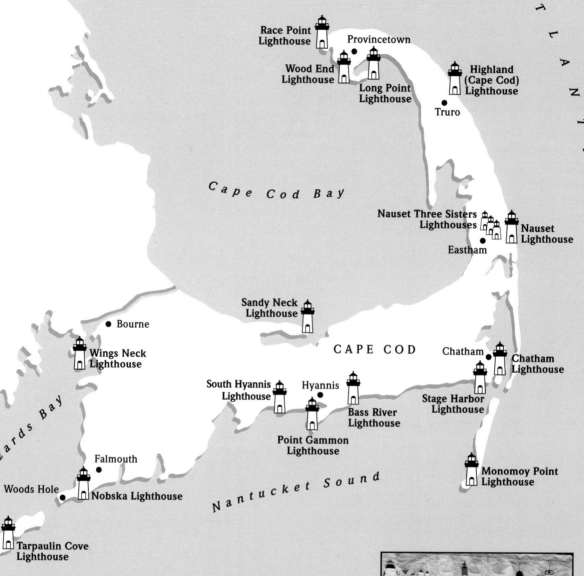

Cape Cod

Race Point
Lighthouse

Provincetown

Wood End
Lighthouse

Long Point
Lighthouse

Highland
(Cape Cod)
Lighthouse

Truro

Cape Cod Bay

ATLANTIC OCEAN

Nauset Three Sisters
Lighthouses

Nauset
Lighthouse

Eastham

Sandy Neck
Lighthouse

Bourne

CAPE COD

Chatham

Chatham
Lighthouse

Wings Neck
Lighthouse

South Hyannis
Lighthouse

Hyannis

Stage Harbor
Lighthouse

Buzzards Bay

Bass River
Lighthouse

Point Gammon
Lighthouse

Falmouth

Monomoy Point
Lighthouse

Woods Hole

Nobska Lighthouse

Nantucket Sound

Tarpaulin Cove
Lighthouse

Wings Neck Light

The peninsula called Wings Neck extends from Pocasset on Cape Cod into Buzzard's Bay, a busy thorofare in the 19th century. The first Wings Neck Light, built in 1848, was a Cape-Cod style structure, with a wooden lantern room atop a stone keeper's house. A Fresnel lens was added in 1856. Although a fire badly damaged the structure in 1878, a new keeper's house and attached octagonal lighthouse were not completed until 1890.

President Warren Harding, in the presidental yacht *Mayflower,* frequently passed near the station and anchored nearby in foul weather. The keeper took note of the anchored yacht and gave the President a 21-gun salute on the station's fog bell.

In 1930 the keeper's house at Ned Point Light in Mattapoisett was floated across Cape Cod to become an assistant keeper's dwelling at Wings Neck. Not long after, however, with the

building of Cleveland Ledge Light, Wings Neck Light was considered expendable. The station was discontinued in 1945 and sold in 1947. The new owners were a musical family and the property became a center of musical activity, including visits from the Trapp family singers.

The lighthouse is on private property; the grounds are not accessible to the public.

C. 1922

Wing Neck Light, Buzzards Bay, Mass.

Directions:

Follow US RT 6 to the Bourne rotary and bear south onto MA 28 heading to Falmouth. At the Wing's Neck/Pocasset sign turn right (west) onto Barlow's Landing Rd. Continue west, crossing County and Shore Roads; bear right onto Wing's Neck Rd. The road divides but either route will take you to a cul-de-sac. The lighthouse may be viewed from the cul-de-sac; there are parking and trespassing restrictions. Cleveland Ledge light is seen in the distance to the southwest offshore.

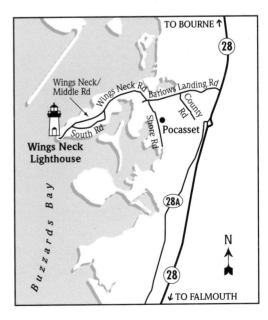

53

Tarpaulin Cove Light

Naushon Island is the largest of the Elizabeth Islands, which extend into Buzzard's Bay in a line from Falmouth on Cape Cod. A beacon was placed on the island by a tavern keeper in 1759 for the "public good of whalemen and coasters". The light was maintained by tavern keepers for 58 years then sold to the federal government in 1817.

In 1817 a 38-foot rubblestone lighthouse tower was built and a Fresnel lens installed in 1856. The tower may also have been rebuilt at that time. The old stone keeper's house was replaced in 1888 and in 1891 a new 28-foot brick lighthouse was built. A fog bell in a tower also was installed; the bell tower was destroyed in the hurricane of 1938.

The light was automated in 1941, after which the house and other buildings fell into disrepair and were torn down in 1962. The Fresnel lens was replaced as well. The island is privately owned and the lighthouse difficult to view closely except by private boat.

Tarpaulin Cove lighthouse "keepers"

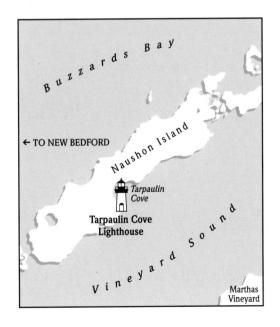

Directions:

The lighthouse is located on Naushon Island off Woods Hole and Martha's Vineyard. It may only be viewed by private boat; the island is privately owned, accessible to residents only.

Buzzards Bay

← TO NEW BEDFORD

Naushon Island

Tarpaulin Cove

Tarpaulin Cove Lighthouse

Vineyard Sound

Marthas Vineyard

Sandy Neck Light

Barnstable was a thriving fishing port and shipyard in the early 19th century. Sandy Neck light was built in 1827 at the west side of the entrance to the harbor, at the tip of the barrier dunes. The first lighthouse was a typical Cape Cod style structure, with a wooden lantern on the roof of a brick keeper's house. In 1857 this lighthouse was replaced by the brick one that still stands; a new Victorian-style keeper's house was built in 1880. In 1887 the cracked brick tower was strengthened with two iron hoops and six staves. This addition is still in place, giving the tower a "distinctive" look.

Because Barnstable harbor was frequently icebound in winter, many crews from trapped

vessels were brought to the light station. However the harbor, virtually inaccessible from January to March, gradually declined in importance and shifting sands left the lighthouse in a less advantageous position. In 1931 the light was decommissioned and the lens moved to a skeleton tower closer to the tip of Sandy Neck. This tower was discontinued in 1952, the lantern room and lens removed and the entire property sold to private ownership.

Sandy Neck light can be seen in the distance from Millway Beach in Barnstable or by boat. Public access to the property is not permitted as it is on the Sandy Neck Wildlife Refuge. Four-wheel drive, permits, and vehicle inspection are required prior to entering the area.

C. 1912

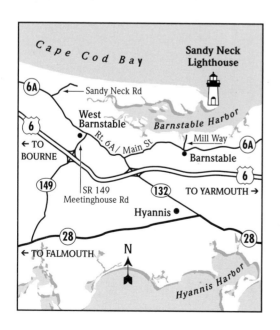

Directions: From US Rt 6 take the MA 149 exit and turn north to Barnstable & West Barnstable. Turn left onto MA 6A (Main Street) and continue to Mill Way. Turn north and continue across a bridge to the dock and beach area. The lighthouse can be seen in the distance across Barnstable Harbor. The lighthouse is most easily photographed by boat. The Sandy Neck area in West Barnstable is a wildlife refuge. There is no public access to the light; permits and four-wheel drive vehicle are required and limited entrance strictly enforced.

Nobska Point Light

Located between Buzzard's Bay and Vineyard Sound, Nobska Point light stands out on the rocky headlands above Woods Hole Harbor. The first lighthouse at Nobska Point was built in 1828, a

typical Cape Cod structure with the octagonal lantern room on top of the keeper's house. In 1876 the light was rebuilt as a 40-foot cast-iron tower lined with brick; a fifth-order Fresnel lens was installed and the new tower painted red. This lighthouse is one of only three lighthouses with miniature brass lighthouses as ornamentation atop each balustrade on the gallery (Cape Neddick and Lubec Channel, both in Maine, are the others). Nobska was upgraded to a fourth-order Fresnel lens in 1888; that lens remains in place.

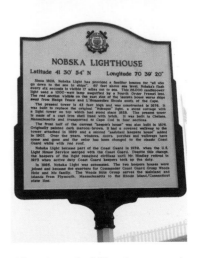

(Continued, following pages)

57

Nobska Point Light

NOBSKA LIGHT, WOODS HOLE, MASS.

The light was automated in 1985 and now serves as the home for the Group Commander of the Woods Hole Coast Guard Base. The lighthouse is easily accessible with a small parking area adjacent; grounds are open to the public. Ferries from Woods Hole to Martha's Vineyard also pass Nobska Point.

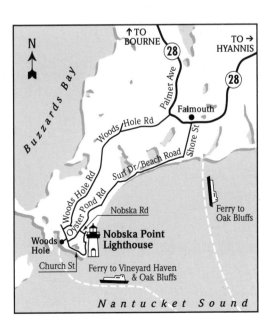

Directions:

Take MA 28 (from the north or east) into Falmouth. Coming from the east: turn south at the intersection of Main St. (MA 28) and Shore St. Follow Shore St./ Surf Dr./Beach Rd. along the shore.; bear left at the intersection with Nobska Rd. and continue to the lighthouse. **Or...**if coming into Falmouth on MA 28 from the north, bear right (west) off MA 28 (Palmer St.) to Woods Hole Rd. Follow the road toward Woods Hole (signs direct you easily). Turn left onto Church St. and follow the road to the lighthouse. Continuing around past the lighthouse, Nobska Rd. joins Oyster Pond Rd.; you've made a loop which leads back to Falmouth. "Vineyard Boat" & "Woods Hole" signs begin well outside Falmouth from all directions and clearly indicate the way.

South Hyannis Light

In the mid 1800s Hyannis Harbor was a busy fishing and trade port and a harbor light was needed to guide mariners into the busy area. The first light was a privately-built shack on the beach, with a lamp hung in a window. Congress then authorized construction of a lighthouse at South Hyannis in

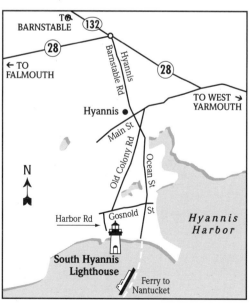

1848 and a small tower was built. A larger lantern room was installed in 1856 to accommodate a Fresnel lens. In 1885 a lamp hoisted atop a 20-foot tower was added on a nearby wharf to serve as a range light. South Hyannis Light was discontinued in 1929 and the entire lantern room removed.

The lighthouse and keeper's dwelling were sold at auction and subsequently passed through various ownership. Current owners have completed extensive restoration of the property but added an unconventional lantern room, now used as a sitting area. Although the light is slightly visible from the street, best views are from excursion boats in the harbor area.

Directions:

At the intersection of MA 132 and MA 28, turn south onto Hyannis/Barnstable Rd(to Hyannis Center). Follow signs to the Nantucket Ferry Ocean St. Dock. Turn south onto Ocean St. and continue to Gosnold St. Turn right, pass Old Colony Rd to the right and continue to Harbor Rd. Turn left, following Harbor Rd. The lighthouse is to your right at the end of the road.

Point Gammon Light

Point Gammon on Great Island is just to the east of the entrance to Hyannis Harbor and about 2.5 miles from the dangerous ledges known as Bishops and Clerks. The fieldstone lighthouse was erected in 1816 in a style unique to New England lighthouses, its stonework and narrow windows suggesting a castle in the British Isles. In 1855 keeper John Peak counted 4,969 schooners, 1,455 sloops, 216 brigs and four steamboats passing his station. Point Gammon light was considered inadequate for this level of traffic, prompting the location of a lightship close to the Bishops and Clerks ledges. In 1858 the lightship was replaced by the Bishops and Clerks lighthouse (now defunct).

Great Island was subsequently sold to private ownership; in 1935 the old stone house was dismantled and the stones used to build a new dwelling on the island. The tower was converted into a summer residence in 1970, with the lantern room refitted as a bedroom; the structure is now empty however. All of the 600-acre Great Island is now private property with no public access. The lighthouse can be viewed distantly from the Hyannis-Nantucket ferry or from fishing and excursion boats leaving Hyannis.

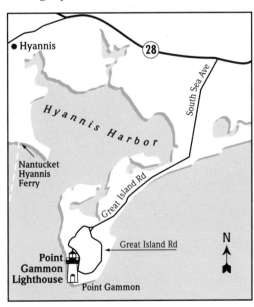

Directions:
The island is privately owned and access is closely restricted; there is no public entrance to the lighthouse. Distant views also are possible from the Hyannis-Nantucket ferries and from the Hyannis to Nantucket flights.

Monomoy Point Light

Extending southward from Chatham at the elbow of Cape Cod's curling arm, Monomoy is at present two islands but was at one time a peninsula connected to the mainland. The area was long a graveyard for vessels due to unusually strong tidal currents. These treacherous currents prompted the Pilgrims to enter Cape Cod Bay, settling at Plymouth rather than continuing on to Virginia.

In the early 19th century a settlement grew up at Monomoy and increased traffic in the area from the fishing industry made a lighthouse necessary. Cape Cod's fifth lighthouse was built at Monomoy Point in 1823, eight miles from Chatham near the southern end of the peninsula. The first lighthouse was a lantern room on the roof of the keeper's house. It appears the lighthouse was rebuilt twice, with the present

cast-iron, brick-lined tower built somewhere between 1855 and 1872; two lifesaving stations also were built in 1872. To make it more visible by day, the tower was painted red in 1882.

With the opening of the Cape Cod Canal in 1914 and an increase in the power of Chatham light, Monomoy light was considered expendable. The light was discontinued in 1923 and the property passed into private ownership. In 1964 the Massachusetts Audubon Society restored the lighthouse and keeper's house; a federal grant funded further refurbishing in 1988.

The Blizzard of 1978 cut Monomoy into two islands--North and South Monomoy--both of which are managed currently by the U.S. Fish and Wildlife Service. The Cape Cod Museum of Natural History offers day trips to the island and overnight stays in the keeper's house.

Directions:

The islands of North and South Monomoy are nine miles south of Chatham; the lighthouse is on the south island. Bird watching trips are offered by the Audubon Society out of Wellfleet ; the Cape Cod Musuem of Natural History also offers trips with overnights possible P.O. Box 1710, Brewster, MA. 1-800-479-3867

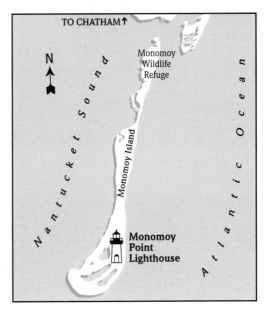

63

Stage Harbor Light

This lighthouse is one of the most recent of the Cape Cod lighthouses. Because the area was busy with fishing traffic and thick fog common, the Lighthouse Board recommended in 1876 that a lighthouse be built on Hardings Beach on the northeast side of the channel known as Chatham Roads. A 48-foot iron tower and wooden keeper's house were completed in 1880 at a cost of $10,000; a fifth-order Fresnel lens was installed.

For a time during prohibition, the floor under the covered walkway between the house and tower became a hiding place for liquor. An inspector on a surprise visit noticed the loose floorboards, but much to the keeper's relief merely advised him to nail them down better. In 1933 an automated light on a skeleton tower replaced Stage Harbor Light. The lantern was removed and the tower capped.

The property is now privately owned. There has never been electricity at the site and no plumbing save a single pump. The lighthouse may be viewed distantly from the harbor; a one-mile walk over sand from Hardings Beach parking area ends at the light.

Directions:

From MA 28 in Chatham/West Chatham, turn south onto Barn Hill Rd. Bear right onto Hardings Beach Rd. and continue to its end at the beach parking area. The lighthouse is about a mile east from the beach along a footpath across the sand dunes.

Alternatively, the lighthouse may be viewed from across Stage Harbor. At the Chatham rotary on MA 28, turn south onto Stage Harbor Rd. and continue south onto Champlain Rd. for about 1.5 miles. Bear left at the intersection of Champlain Rd. and Battlefield Rd. into Sears Rd. Turn left onto Sears Point Rd. and continue for approximately 0.5mile to the road's end at a public boat landing.

65

Bass River Light

The Bass River Lighthouse, now the Lighthouse Inn, barely resembles the original structure built in 1855; only the lantern room on the roof remains visible amid the additions.

In 1850 Congress appropriated $4,000 for a lighthouse in West Dennis to guide vessels through Nantucket Sound. Until this time a man named William Crowell kept a lantern burning in his attic window to aid local mariners; ship captains paid for his lantern oil by donating 25 cents a month. When the lighthouse was completed Crowell appropriately became the first keeper and remained in the position until 1880 save for a nine-year stint in the Union army during the Civil War.

Bass River light was discontinued in 1880 and sold at auction after the lighting of Stage Harbor light in Chatham. Six months later complaints caused the government to buy the lighthouse back, relighting it in 1881. However, with the advent of the Cape Cod Canal and installation of an

automated beacon at the entrance to Bass River, the lighthouse was considered unnecessary. The light was extinguished in 1914 and its fourth-order Fresnel lens removed.

The property passed into private ownership and was opened as the Lighthouse Inn in 1938. In 1989 the light was reactivated as a private aid to navigation with a 300mm optic providing assistance to local mariners.

Directions:
On MA 28 in West Dennis, turn south onto School St. (just east of the Bass River Bridge). Continue to Lighthouse Road and turn right; it is about 0.5 mile to the Lighthouse Inn Road. Turn left and continue to the parking lot at the inn. There is a paved path on the east side of the inn that leads to a seawall.

Chatham Light

Established in 1808, Chatham light station was intended to give Cape Cod a second lighthouse to assist mariners making the difficult trip from Nantucket Sound around the Cape. The obvious choice for this light was Chatham, at the elbow of Cape Cod's crooked "arm".

To distinguish Chatham from Highland Light, it was decided to make Chatham a twin light station. The first octagonal twin towers were built of wood, each one 40 feet high, about 70 feet apart. A small one-bedroom dwelling also was built; Samuel Nye was appointed first keeper by President Thomas Jefferson. The twin lights had six lamps each, with 8.5 inch parabolic reflectors and green glass lenses. This system, the Argand lamp, was devised by Winslow Lewis. Although an efficient system, the reflective coating quickly wore off with repeated polishings and the green lenses diminished the lights' brightness. Nevertheless Winslow's system was used for several decades in American lighthouses.

The first Chatham twin lights lasted 33 years, then were replaced by 40-foot brick towers, built further from the rapidly eroding cliff. In 1857 both lights received fourth-order Fresnel lenses, each showing a fixed white light.

By 1877, erosion from storms had "relocated" the Chatham lights from 228 feet to only 48 feet from the edge of a 50-foot cliff. In December 1879 the south tower fell to the beach below; 15 months later the keeper's house and north tower met the same fate. However, two years prior to the 1877 demise of the lights, the optics had been moved to a third pair of lights. The new towers were built of iron plates, lined with brick; the present keeper's house was built at this time.

(Continued, following pages)

In 1923 the Chatham north light was moved to Eastham's Nauset Beach to replace the Three Sisters Lighthouses, thus ending 115 years of twin lights at Chatham. A new rotating optic was placed in the remaining tower along with an incandescent oil vapor lens. In 1939 the Coast Guard electrified the light, increasing its intensity from 30,000 to 800,000 candlepower. The Fresnel lens and entire lantern room were removed from the Chatham light in 1969 when aero beacons were installed, producing a rotating 2.8 million candlepower light visible for 25 miles. A new, larger lantern room was constructed to accommodate the new optics. The old lantern room and lens are on the grounds of the Chatham Historical Society.

The light was automated in 1982; the keeper's dwelling is used for Coast Guard housing and offices associated with the Coast Guard Station. The monument standing near the foundaton of the old north light was erected in memory of seven members of the Monomoy Life Saving Station who died in a resue attempt in 1902.

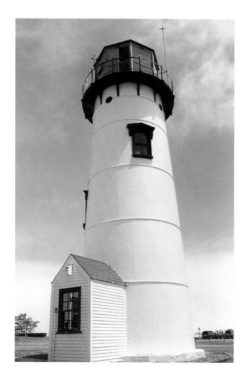

View from the lantern room

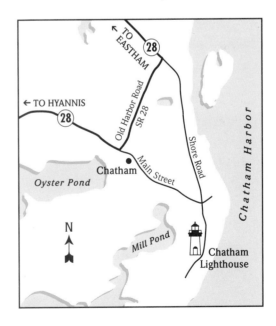

Directions:

At the Chatham rotary on MA 28, bear southeast onto Main Street. At the T-intersection with Shore Rd. bear right to the lighthouse and coast guard station. There is parking across the street from the lighthouse.

Nauset Light & The Three Sisters

In 1837 the government decided to establish a lighthouse station at Nauset Beach, on the back shore of Cape Cod halfway between Highland (Cape Cod) Light and the twin lights at Chatham. The decision was not entirely met with enthusiasm as "wrecking" (salvaging materials from wrecked ships) had been a major industry on the Cape for some time. A lighthouse, area residents claimed, would significantly hurt local "business".

To differentiate the new station from its neighbors (Highland and Chatham), a unique plan was devised. Three identical lighthouses were built 150 feet apart, the only "triplet" lighthouses in U.S. history; a one-story keeper's house was also built. The nickname "Three Sisters of Nauset" quickly followed.

Original lens, now at the Eastham visitors center

During relocation, 1997

By 1890 the Three Sisters stood close to the edge of the bluff and in 1892 three new wooden towers were built further back from the cliff. Fourth-order Fresnel lenses were added, along with a new keeper's house and oil house. In 1911 Nauset was changed to a single light; the center lighthouse was again moved back from the bluff and the two other towers removed and sold.

In 1923 Chatham became a single-light station and the discontinued twin was relocated to Nauset Beach; the keeper's house was moved back next to the new tower. The final Sister was subsequently sold to private owners. The Nauset became a familiar Cape Cod icon and trademark logo when the top half of the white cast-iron tower was painted red in 1940.

The lighthouse prior to relocation from the eroding shoreline

Nauset light was automated in 1955, the Fresnel lens replaced by aerobeacons and the characteristic changed to alternating red and white flashes. The Coast Guard proposed the decommissioning of the lighthouse in 1993 as erosion had almost completely destroyed the cliff just east of the tower. The Nauset Light Preservation Society was formed, spearheaded by local residents, and in 1995 a long-term lease was granted for the lighthouse. Federal grant money and individual contributions funded the move to the present site in the fall of 1996. Negotiations are ongoing for relocation of the keeper's house; the light will now be a private aid to navigation.

The old Fresnel lens is on display at the Cape Cod National Seashore Visitors Center in Eastham. The keeper's house is now privately owned.

After relocation to the new site

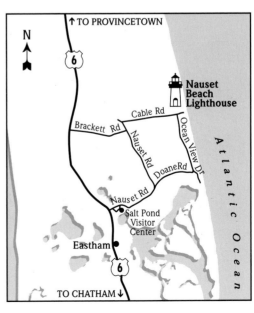

Directions:
See directions for the Three Sisters, following page.

71

First Sister

Second Sister

Third Sister

The Three Sisters

The National Park Service has purchased and restored the Three Sisters at their original configuration at a site about one-third mile from the Nauset light. A well-marked path leads from the beach parking area to the small park.

Directions: (For Nauset Light & Three Sisters)

Follow RT 6 into Eastham and turn east on Brackett Rd. (marked with "Nauset Beach Light" sign). Continue to Nauset Rd. and turn left, then bear right onto Cable St. Continue to the road's end at the intersection with Ocean View Drive and beach parking area. Across Ocean View Dr. there is a marked path leading to the restored lighthouses.

Or.. From RT 6 turn right at a "Cape Cod National Seashore" sign onto Nauset/Salt Pond Rd. Pass the Salt Pond Visitor Center and continue on to Ocean View Dr. Turn left at that intersection and continue to the Nauset Beach parking area.

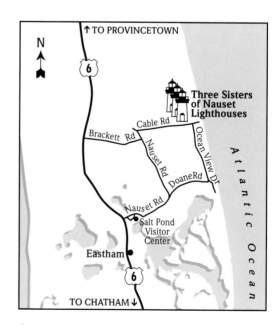

72

Highland (Cape Cod) Light

A preponderance of shipwrecks at the "High Land" prompted the Boston Marine Society recommendation in the late 1700s that a lighthouse be built at this location in North Truro. In 1791 a 30-foot brick lighthouse was built 500 feet from the edge of the bluff. To avoid confusion with Boston Light, Highland Light became the first lighthouse in the nation with a flashing light.

One of the worst wrecks near the light was that of the British bark *Josephus* in 1852. Keeper Enoch Hamilton returned hours after the wreck to find that two of the 16 crew members had washed ashore and survived. One of the survivors, John Jasper, later became the captain of an ocean liner; when his vessel passed Highland light he would dip the flag as a signal of respect to the keeper.

A new Highland light was built in 1857 and equipped with a first-order Fresnel lens. This powerful light made Highland one of the coast's most powerful; it was also the highest on the New England mainland. In 1901 an even larger Fresnel lens, floating on a bed of mercury, was installed. When an electric light was put inside this lens in 1932 Highland then became the coast's most powerful beacon. The four million candlepower light was visible for 45 miles (reportedly for 75 miles in clear weather).

C. 1917

73

Highland Light

In the early 1950s the giant lens was removed and replaced by aerobeacons; the light was automated in 1986 and the keeper's house used for Coast Guard housing. The lighthouse now belongs to the National Park Service and is considered a private aid to navigation. Signs on Cape Cod Route 6 direct you to the lighthouse, now located at the Highland Golf Links; parking is available at the area.

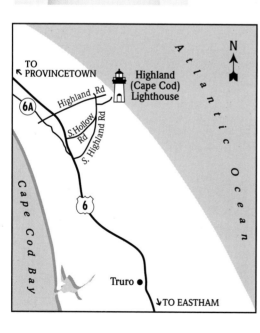

Directions:

Take US Rt 6 to North Truro; turn east at the "Highland (Cape Cod) Light" sign and follow Highland Road to a T-intersection with South Highland Rd. Turn right and follow South Highland to Lighthouse Rd., turn left at the entrance to the Cape Cod lighthouse (marked) and Highland Golf Links. There is a parking area at the light. It is now possible to walk all around the lighthouse since its relocation in the fall of 1996. Because the lighthouse is located on the golf course, following signs to "Highland Golf Links" also bring you to the lighthouse.

74

MOVING A LIGHTHOUSE

The first Highland lighthouse was built 500 feet from the edge of a 125-foot cliff. Erosion claimed at least three feet of the cliff per year until, by the early 1990s, the lighthouse stood a little more than 100 feet from the edge. In 1990 alone, 40 feet were lost just north of the lighthouse.

A group within the Truro Historical Society began fund raising for relocation of the light. Donations from local residents and tourists, coupled with sales of Highland Light memorabilia, raised $150,000. In 1996, this money combined with National Park Service, state and Coast Guard funds totalled $1.5 million, the amount needed for relocation of the 404-ton lighthouse to a site 450 feet back from its original location.

The operation got underway in June 1996 and took 18 days to complete. The relocated lighthouse now stands close to the seventh fairway of the Highland Golf Links. On Sunday, November 7, 1996 Highland Light was relighted amid pomp and ceremony.

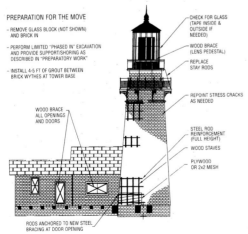

PREPARATION FOR THE MOVE

– REMOVE GLASS BLOCK (NOT SHOWN) AND BRICK IN

– PERFORM LIMITED "PHASED IN" EXCAVATION AND PROVIDE SUPPORT/SHORING AS DESCRIBED IN "PREPARATORY WORK"

– INSTALL 4-5 FT OF GROUT BETWEEN BRICK WYTHES AT TOWER BASE

CHECK FOR GLASS (TAPE INSIDE & OUTSIDE IF NEEDED)

WOOD BRACE (LENS PEDESTAL)

REPLACE STAY RODS

REPOINT STRESS CRACKS AS NEEDED

STEEL ROD REINFORCEMENT (FULL HEIGHT)

WOOD STAVES

PLYWOOD OR 2x2 MESH

WOOD BRACE ALL OPENINGS AND DOORS

RODS ANCHORED TO NEW STEEL BRACING AT DOOR OPENING

***Plans for the relocation of the lighthouse.
International Chimney, contractors***

Wood End Light

The 39-foot square brick tower that still stands at Wood End was built in 1872, making it the youngest lighthouse in the area. The lighthouse originally was painted brown and exhibited a red flashing light. In 1896 a second wooden keeper's house was added, along with an oil house. A fog bell in a tower was added near the light in 1902.

Duty at this station had its unique drawbacks as the keeper in 1880 complained of the "stench and flies coming from the fish-oil works" between Wood End and Long Point, a mile away. Also notable was the 1927 collision of a Navy submarine and Coast Guard cutter eight days before Christmas one-half mile south of Wood End light; 42 men perished in the disaster.

The lighthouse was automated in 1961 with all outbuildings except the oil house destroyed. The fifth-order Fresnel lens was removed and replaced by an aerobeacon; the light was converted to solar power in 1981. It is possible to walk across the breakwater, then over sand to the lighthouse, although at high tide several low points are covered with water, making the route tricky. Excursion boats and whale watches also pass by this light.

Wood End Light, Provincetown, Mass.

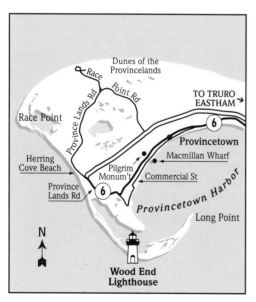

Directions:

The light can be seen in the distance from the Pilgrim's Landing Plaque area at the end of Commercial Street (one way), opposite the breakwater that extends to the lighthouse. Whale watching cruises from Provincetown pass close to this light and offer good views. To walk to the lighthouse, park at the breakwater at the end of Commercial St. The breakwater is about 1/2 mile long; the lighthouse is another 1/2 mile to your right over sand. Be prepared for a strenuous walk; you will be crossing through water at several points unless the tide is dead low.

Long Point Light, Provincetown, Mass.

Long Point Light

At the fingertip of the curling arm of Cape Cod, Long Point was a settlement of about 200 people in the 1800s, boasting a school and sea salt industry. Provincetown had become a major fishing port and it was decided a lighthouse at Long Point would aid mariners entering the harbor. In 1827 the first lighthouse was completed and consisted of a lantern room atop the keeper's house; a sixth-order Fresnel lens was installed in 1856.

During the Civil War a Confederate warship was seen near Provincetown, prompting the construction of two forts at Long Point, close to the lighthouse. Local residents called the batteries "Fort Useless" and "Fort Harmless"; no shots were ever fired.

A new 38-foot brick lighthouse and keeper's house were built in 1875 with a fog bell and fifth-order Fresnel lens installed at that time. Long Point light was automated in 1952 and the Fresnel lens replaced; solar panels were added in 1982. The keeper's house and fog signal building were destroyed. The lighthouse can be seen in the distance from MacMillan Wharf in Provincetown; various boats leaving Provincetown pass close by the light. Walking to the lighthouse is possible but involves crossing an uneven 1/2-mile long breakwater, then an additional mile over sand to the point, crossing through water unless at dead low tide.

Directions:

From US Route 6, take either of the exits west into Provincetown and head to MacMillan Wharf. Provincetown is a congested area with narrow streets; parking is available at the wharf and all whale watching cruises depart from that area. Long Point light can be seen from the wharf; the whale watching excursions all pass close to this light. To walk to the lighthouse, park at the breakwater at the end of Commercial St. The breakwater is about 1/2 mile long; the lighthouse is another mile to your left over sand to Long Point. Be prepared for a strenuous walk; you will be crossing through water at several points unless the tide is dead low.

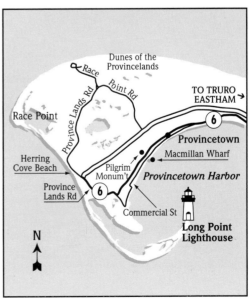

77

Race Point Light

Countless shipwrecks occured in the area of Race Point at the northern tip of Cape Cod throughout the 18th century, as all vessels travelling between Boston and points south had to negotiate the treacherous bars off the point. As early as 1808 the people of Provincetown asked for a lighthouse at Race Point; the first was built in 1816. The rubblestone tower's revolving light was an attempt to differentiate it from the other lighthouses on the Cape, and one of the earliest of this design.

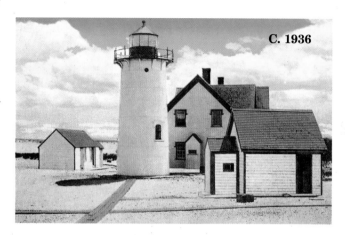

C. 1936

In 1852 a fog bell was installed and three years later a fourth-order Frensel lens added. The fog bell was replaced in 1873 with a steam-driven fog signal housed in a new building. The old stone tower was replaced with a 45-foot cast iron structure, lined with brick; the Fresnel lens was moved and changed from flashing white to fixed. Three keepers and their families lived in two separate keeper's houses; the children's walk to school was 2.5 miles over sand each day, each way.

Despite the help afforded by the lighthouse, lives continued to be lost in the Race Point vicinity. During the period 1890 to 1903 there were 28 major shipping disasters in the area. The infamous Portland Gale of 1898 claimed more than 500 lives, 200 on the steamer *Portland*. Pieces of some wrecks continue to appear occasionally in the area as the sands shift.

During the early 1800s a sizeable fishing community and saltworks flourished at Race Point. The small community, known as "Helltown" even declared a separate school district in the 1830s. However, the latter part of the 19th century saw the fishing settlement dwindle.

Race Point light was electrified in 1957 and three years later the larger keeper's house razed.The light was automated in 1978, a new optic replaced the Fresnel lens and solar power subsequently installed. Now on the grounds of the Cape Cod Nationsl Seashore, the surrounding property, keeper's house and oil house were leased to the New England Lighthouse Foundation. Repairs and restoration to the interior and exterior were completed in 1997. The group hopes to offer overnight stays in the keeper's house.

Parking is available at Race Point Beach. The walk to the light is strenuous, two miles over sand. A four-wheel drive vehicle and permit are required for access to the restricted area. Dune tours are possible in the summer months.

Race Point Light, Provincetown, Mass.   20

Directions:

Take the Race Point exit from Route 6 and follow the road through the Provincelands park area. Bear right at the Provincetown Airport and pass the visitors center. The road ends in a parking area at Race Point Beach. The lighthouse is a two-mile walk over sand from the parking area. Access is possible with four-wheel drive vehicle but an over-sand permit and check in is required. Alternatively, the light can be seen at a distance from the parking area at Herring Cove Beach. Whale watching cruises from Provincetown pass close to this light and offer good views.

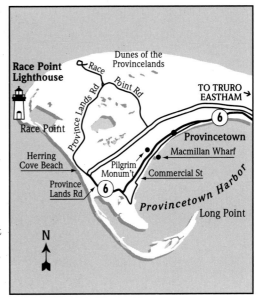

The Southeast Shore

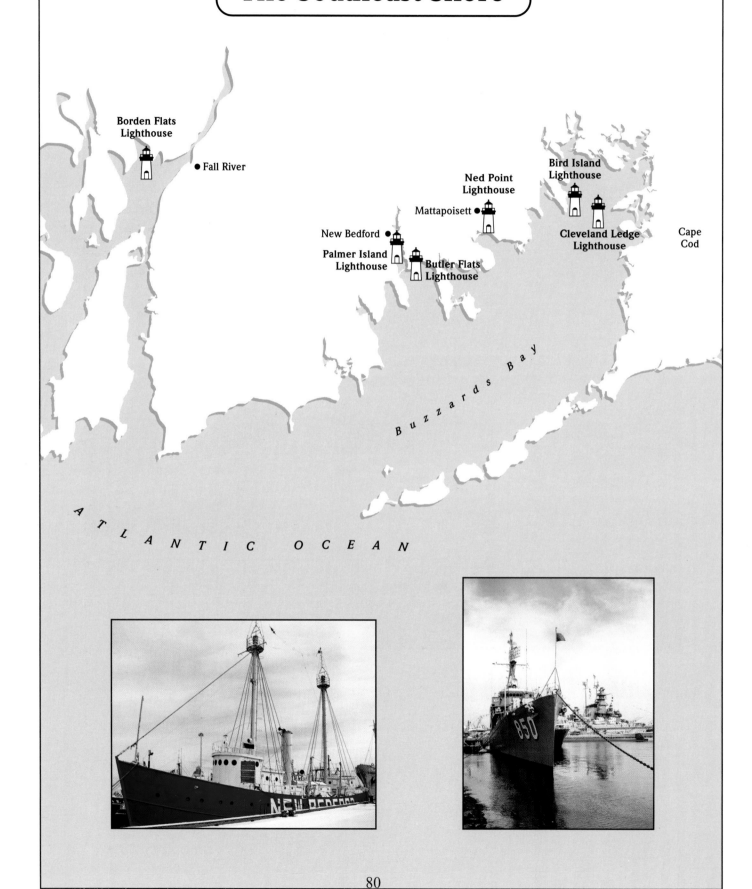

Borden Flats
Lighthouse

● Fall River

New Bedford ●

Palmer Island
Lighthouse

Butler Flats
Lighthouse

Mattapoisett ●

Ned Point
Lighthouse

Bird Island
Lighthouse

Cleveland Ledge
Lighthouse

Cape
Cod

Buzzards Bay

ATLANTIC OCEAN

Borden Flats Light

The city of Fall River is famous as the home town of Lizzie Borden, who was acquitted of the ax murder of her father and stepmother. Borden Flats Light was named for Lizzie's family, one of the most prominent in Fall River, years before the murders.

Built in 1881 near the Braga Bridge crossing the Taunton River, Borden Flats light is built entirely of cast iron plates on a concrete caisson base. The lighthouse received a fourth-order Fresnel lens. After being battered in the Hurricane of 1938 (as were most lighthouses on New England's south-facing coast), a new, wider cylindrical caisson was built around the old one. A cistern is on the first level, with five stories above, two of which were used as living quarters.

Borden Flats light was automated in 1963 and in 1977 its Fresnel lens was replaced by a modern plastic lens. The lighthouse can be seen easily from the bridge and shore points in Fall River.

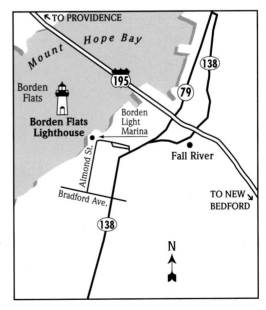

Directions:
From I-195 or Rt 24 take MA 138 South (Broadway) into Fall River. Turn west onto Bradford St. then right onto Almond St. Follow Almond St. to the dead end at Park Street and turn into the Borden Light Marina; the lighthouse is to the west of the marina.

Palmer Island Light

New Bedford was the whaling capital of the nation in the mid-nineteenth century and in 1849 a lighthouse was built on the northern point of Palmer Island on the west side of the entrance to the harbor. The 24-foot tower was built of rubble-stone with wooden windows and floors.

In the 1860s a hotel and dance hall were built on the southern side of Palmer Island. The hotel was a favorite stop for returning whalers; not surprisingly illegal activity also flourished. An amusement park was built in 1890 but it soon failed and the hotel burned in 1905.

The island has been the scene of great heroism and tragedy, in particular the tale of keeper Arthur Small. On September 21, 1938, the worst hurricane in New England history battered the south-facing coast. That afternoon Small left for the lighthouse, a 350-foot walk from the keeper's house and was struck by a sudden tidal wave. He looked back to see his wife attempting to launch a rowboat to reach him. Small somehow made it back to the tower to tend the light; Mabel Small did not survive.

The lighthouse was automated in 1941 but with the construction of a massive hurricane wall in New Bedford harbor in the 1960s, the light was deemed unnecessary. In 1966 the tower was burned by arsonists; renovations in 1989 were soon lost to futher vandalism. Today Palmer Island is littered with debris, the lighthouse an empty shell and the lantern room empty. Ironically the lighthouse is featured on the city seal of New Bedford with the motto "I Spread the Light." The light is accessible at low tide from the hurricane wall.

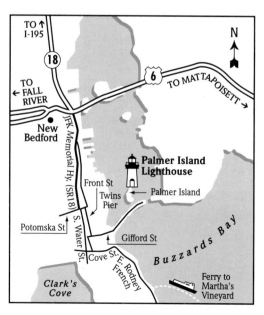

Directions:

From I-195 in New Bedford, take the MA 18 (Downtown) exit south. Continue on MA 18 south to Cove St. and turn left;follow Cove St. to its end at the hurricane wall and bear right. Park along a side street or in marked lots and walk up along the wall back north. A paved path continues to the right and leads to the island which can be accessed at low tide. **Alternatively..** turn left onto Potomska St. from MA 18, then right onto Front St. At Gifford St. turn left and continue to a parking lot behind industrial buildings.

Butler Flats Light

Built in shallow water without solid rock for foundation, Butler Flats light was a challenge to construct in 1898 to replace Clark's Point Light. An iron cylinder 35 feet in diameter was placed then filled with stone and concrete; the brick lighthouse was built on top. The sparkplug-style light, similar in appearance to Boston's Deer Island Light, has four stories and originally had a fifth-order Fresnel lens. Butler Flats had only three keepers from its first lighting until 1942 when the Coast Guard took over from the Lighthouse Service.

In 1975 a new automatic light and fog signal were placed on New Bedford's hurricane barrier and the lighthouse was deemed unnecessary. It was automated and became one of the first solar-powered lighthouses. After decommissioning in 1978 the light came under control of the City of New Bedford and a private group took responsibility for maintenance of the light. Best views of Butler Flats are from the New Bedford-Martha's Vineyard ferry.

Directions:

From I-195 or US RT 6 in New Bedford, take MA 18 south; continue on MA 18/Water St. to Cove Rd. Turn left (east) onto Cove Rd. Bear right at the intersection with East Rodney French, passing the New Bedford ferry terminal. Continue to the intersection with Ricketson St; the seawall just south of Ricketson St. affords best views. Parking is restricted along East Rodney French, but not along the side streets. There are free parking lots closeby. The light is best photographed from the ferry to Martha's Vineyard.

New Bedford Ferry: Turn left off East Rodney French at Norman St. The ferry runs daily late May through Columbus Day; crossing time is about 90 minutes. **Cape Island Express Lines, Inc., P.O. Box J-405, New Bedford, MA 02741 (508) 997-1688.**

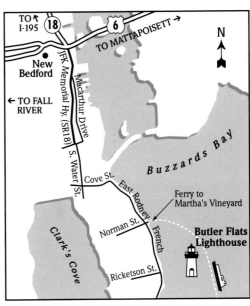

Ned Point Light

The first lighthouse at Ned Point, at the northeast side of the entrance to Mattapoisett Harbor on Buzzard's Bay, was a 35-foot rubblestone tower built in 1837 at a cost of $4500. The construction was not yet complete when an inspector arrived, so the contractor took him to the nearby tavern he owned while workers attempted to make the structure appear finished. The ruse failed however, when the inspector stepped on loose planking, falling into the foundation of the tower.

A new 39-foot tower was built in 1888 and a fifth-order Fresnel lens added. The keeper's house was removed in 1930 and floated by barge across Buzzard's Bay to Wing's Neck Light in Bourne. Legend has it that the last keeper made the trip in the house, cooking breakfast along the way across the bay.

The Coast Guard decommissioned Ned Point light in 1952; the site surrounding the tower was sold to the Town of Mattapoisett in 1958 and developed into a park. The light was reactivated in 1961.

Ned point is a popular spot for weddings and engagements, with the lighthouse as backdrop. The Coast Guard repainted and refurbished the tower in 1995, installing a new optic as well. The area and lighthouse are well-tended and easily accessible.

Ned Point Light, Mattapoisett, Mass.

C. 1909

Directions:

From I-195 (north):Take the Mattapoisett exit and follow North Street into town. Turn east (left) onto Water St; continue on Water St./Beacon St. to Ned Point Rd. and bear right. Follow Ned Point Rd. for about 0.5 mile to Ned Point and the light. **From US Rt 6** (from Cape Cod or New Bedford): Continue into Mattapoisett and turn east onto Water St. Follow Water St./Beacon St. to Ned Point Rd. and bear right. Follow Ned Point Rd. for about 0.5 mile to Ned Point and the light. There is a park with picnic tables and parking area at the lighthouse.

Bird Island Light

Located in Sippican Harbor, near the town of Marion, the first Bird Island light was built in 1819. The 25-foot rubblestone tower was one of the first lighthouses of that time to receive a revolving optic.

Local legend says that the first keeper, William Moore, was a pirate, banished to Bird Island as punishment. However, others note that his letters during that time mention a boat and his work on various inventions, casting doubt that Mr. Moore was a pirate-prisoner. Some accounts further claim that Moore murdered his wife at the lighthouse and disappeared soon thereafter. A gun reportedly was found in a secret hiding place when the original keeper's house was razed; some believe it was the murder weapon. Keeper Moore denied the charges, claiming the effects of tobacco caused his wife's death. Although she is supposedly buried on the island, there is no sign of the grave.

In 1889 the rubblestone tower was refurbished and equipped with a flashing fourth-order Fresnel lens; a new keeper's house was subsequently added. The last keeper at Bird Island (1919-1926) was Maurice Babcock who later became the last civilian keeper at Boston Light. The lighthouse was taken out of service in June 1935 as ship traffic in the area had diminished greatly. Every building on Bird Island except the lighthouse tower was destroyed by the Hurrican of '38; some local residents claim to have seen the stations fog bell being swept off the island in the storm.

In 1939 the island was sold to private ownership and since 1966 the property has been owned by the town of Marion. The Town of Marion and Sippican Historical Society raised $13,000 for repairs to the lighthouse and on July 9, 1976 Bird Island light was relighted as a private aid to navigation. Vandals damaged the optic in 1981 rendering the light nonfunctional. In 1994 a new effort to restore the light was mounted by the Bird Island Preservation Society. Private funds and federal grants enabled restoration of the lighthouse tower and Bird Island Light was relit as a private aid to navigation on July 4, 1997; the optic is solar powered.

The island is now considered an important nesting site for common terns and endangered roseate terns. Although visible distantly from shore, the light is best viewed by boat.

Directions:

From I-195: Take the MA 105 exit south (becomes Front/ Rochester St.); continue to US Rt 6 and turn north (left). Go about 1.5 miles to Butler Point/Point Rd and turn south. Continue on this road across Sippican Neck to the road's end at a golf course. The lighthouse can be seen in the distance from along the seawall.

From US 6: From Marion, continue north about 1.5 miles past the intersection with MA 105 (Front/Rochester St.). Turn south onto Butler Point/Point Rd. and follow the road to it's end at the golf course.From Wareham, continue south to to "MarionTown Limit" sign and go approximately 0.5 mile to the intersection of Rt 6 and Butler Point/Point Rd. Turn south onto Butler Point/Point Rd. and follow the road to it's end at the golf course.

Cleveland Ledge Light

At the western entrance to the Cape Cod Canal, Cleveland Ledge Light is the last commissioned lighthouse built in New England and the only one built by the Coast Guard. The project was started by the state of Massachusetts in 1940 then transferred to the federal government in 1941 and finished in 1943. Cleveland Ledge was named for President Grover Cleveland who frequently fished in the area.The style of this lighthouse is unique among New England lighthouses, having been described as "uncharacteristic of any frugal, Yankee heritage." A 50-foot tower sits atop two stories that were used as living and work quarters; the entire structure sits on a 52-foot cylindrical caisson pier.

On September 14,1944 a hurricane battered the lighthouse, dislodging a glass block skylight and allowing water to wash through the structure. The nine-man crew had to bail water from the engine room as the water level neared the batteries which powered the station. Fortunately the water stopped rising about two inches below the batteries, allowing the light to continue flashing throughout the storm.

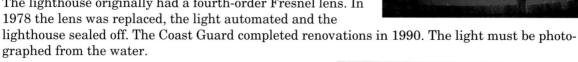

The lighthouse originally had a fourth-order Fresnel lens. In 1978 the lens was replaced, the light automated and the lighthouse sealed off. The Coast Guard completed renovations in 1990. The light must be photographed from the water.

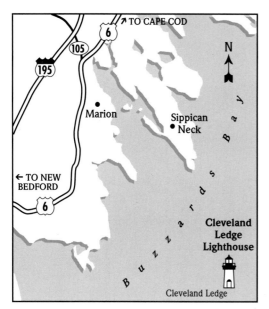

88

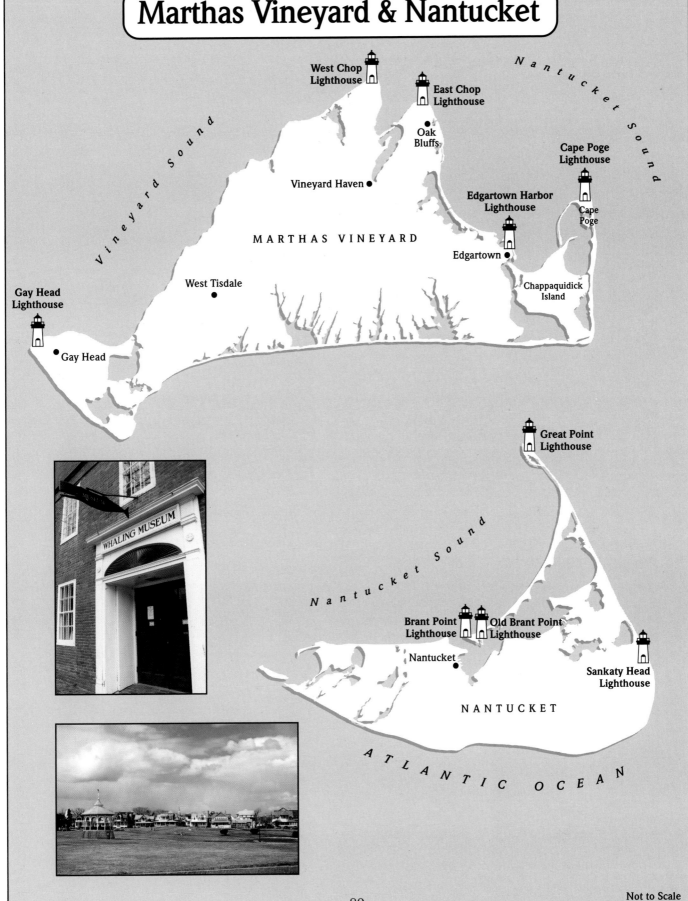

Marthas Vineyard & Nantucket

West Chop
Lighthouse

East Chop
Lighthouse

N a n t u c k e t   S o u n d

Oak
Bluffs

Cape Poge
Lighthouse

V i n e y a r d   S o u n d

Vineyard Haven

Edgartown Harbor
Lighthouse

Cape
Poge

MARTHAS VINEYARD

Edgartown

Gay Head
Lighthouse

West Tisdale

Chappaquidick
Island

Gay Head

WHALING MUSEUM

Great Point
Lighthouse

N a n t u c k e t   S o u n d

Brant Point
Lighthouse

Old Brant Point
Lighthouse

Nantucket

Sankaty Head
Lighthouse

NANTUCKET

A T L A N T I C   O C E A N

Not to Scale

West Chop Light

The harbor at Vineyard Haven on Martha's Vineyard is protected by two areas of land known as East Chop and West Chop. The first 25-foot stone tower at West Chop was built in 1817; the town was then called Holmes Hole and the light often referred to as Holmes Hole Light. In 1843 inspection found the house in poor condition and the decision was made to build a new house and rubble-stone tower in 1846, almost 1000 feet southeast of the original location.

Three range lights were added in 1854, replaced in 1856 by a range light on the keeper's house which was then discontinued in 1859. A steam-driven fog signal was added in 1882; an assistant keeper's house also was built during that year.

By 1891 the proliferation of large homes in the area began to obscure the light and a 17-foot mast with the light on top was added. Soon after, the tower was replaced by a new 45-foot brick tower, painted red. The new West Chop light was painted white in 1896. The light was automated in 1976 but the original fourth-order Fresnel lens remains in place. The Vineyard Environmental Research Institute uses the buildings at the station for offices. The lighthouse can be seen from West Chop Road and on entering Vineyard Haven harbor on the ferries.

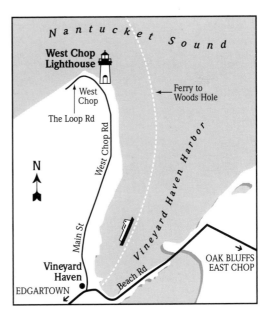

Directions:

From the Vineyard Haven ferry landing, turn right onto Main St. and continue to West Chop Rd. Follow West Chop Rd. (becomes one way) to the lighthouse. Parking is possible on the street, NOT in the drive. Continuing past the lighthouse the road becomes Loop Rd. which eventually winds around back into Vineyard Haven . **From Oak Bluffs**, follow Beach Rd. into Vineyard Haven, then take Main St./West Chop Rd. to the lighthouse. Bus tours of the island also are available from the Vineyard Haven ferry landing but these are not primarily lighthouse tours.

C. 1967

East Chop Light

In 1869 Captain Silas Daggett erected a lighthouse at East Chop, the eastern point of Vineyard Haven harbor, and operated it privately for seven years. Donations from local merchants paid for upkeep of the light. This structure burned in 1871 but Dagget rebuilt it as a light atop a house.

The government purchased the land and lighthouse in 1878 and built a new keeper's house and present cast-iron lighthouse.

Directions:

From Vineyard Haven ferry landing, bear left onto Beach Rd. ; follow the "East Chop Light" signs, bearing left onto Eastville Ave. then right onto East Chop Dr./Highland Dr. Continue along the shore to the light. From Oak Bluffs, follow Oak Bluffs Drive to East Chop Drive. Turn right and follow East Chop Dr./Highland Dr. to the light. The lighthouse is at a park area with limited street parking.

The keeper's house and oil house were removed in 1934 when the station was automated. The original Fresnel lens was replaced by a plastic lens in 1984. From 1962 to 1984 the lighthouse was painted a reddish-brown, earning it the nickname "Chocolate Lighthouse". Today only the tower remains, painted a more traditional white and exhibiting a three-second green flash, visible for 15 miles.

In 1986 the Vineyard Environmental Research Institute became responsible for the maintenance of East Chop light. The license was transferred to the Dukes County Historical Society in 1993, along with licenses for Gay Head and Edgartown Harbor lights. The Society periodically opens the lights to the public in summer months.

Oak Bluffs

93

Gay Head Light

Built in 1798 to aid mariners entering Vineyard Sound from Buzzard's Bay, Gay Head lighthouse stands in one of the most picturesque locations in New England, atop the 130-foot multi-colored clay cliffs at the western shore of Martha's Vineyard. The original octagonal lighthouse was first lighted in November 1799.

In 1838 the lantern and deck were rebuilt; subsequently conflicting reports and recommendations were submitted regarding the visibility of the light. Finally, in 1854, a new, 51-foot brick lighthouse was built to house a first-order Fresnel lens which contained 1008 prisms.

However, despite the new, powerful light, shipwrecks continued to happen regularly in the vicinity.The worst of these disasters occurred in the early morning of January 19, 1884 when the passenger steamer *City of Columbus* ran aground on Devil's Bridge, a treacherous ledge near the Gay Head Cliffs. Twenty minutes later 100 people on board had drowned. Fortunately some managed to hold onto the rigging long enough for the lighthouse keeper to arrive in a lifeboat with a crew of Gay Head Indians. The wreck of the *City of Columbus* remains among New England's worst marine disasters.

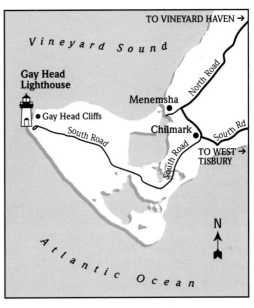

The brick keeper's house was torn down in 1856 as it was thought to be the extreme dampness of the house which was causing an often fatal mysterious illness. In 1902 a new wooden structure was built on a much higher foundation so it would remain dry. In 1952 the old Fresnel lens was replaced by a modern automatic light.

The lens can be seen today on the grounds of the Dukes County Historical Society in Edgartown. Today only the lighthouse tower remains at Gay Head; it is easily accessible by car with parking available at a scenic lookout area.The Historical Society periodically opens the lighthouse: **(508) 627-4441.**

Directions:

Follow appropriate signs to West Tisbury and Chilmark--you will be following North Rd. (from Vineyard Haven) or South Road (from West Tisbury). At Chilmark continue on South Rd. to Gay Head; signs clearly indicate the route to Gay Head. The lighthouse is at the road's end. A parking and refreshment area is available.

Edgartown Harbor Light

Martha's Vineyard had a prosperous whaling industry in the early 19th century and the harbor at Edgartown was one of the island's most protected. In 1828 the government purchased land and a two-story house with lantern on the roof was built for about $4000. The fixed white light was visible for 14 miles. This type of lighthouse structure was commonly known as "Cape Cod style"; today no such structures survive on Cape Cod save the much-changed Bass River lighthouse.

Edgartown Harbor light was located offshore on a stone pier; in 1830 a causeway was built to the lighthouse. The walkway became known locally as the "Bridge of Sighs" because men about to leave on whaling voyages often strolled there with girlfriends or wives.

The lighthouse and walkway were damaged and repaired many times but the Hurricane of '38 was the final blow and in 1939 the Coast Guard demolished Edgartown Light. Plans were to erect a beacon on a skeleton tower but objections from residents prompted an alternate plan: relocation of an 1873 cast iron tower from Crane's Beach in Ipswich. The 45-foot tower received an automatic light flashing red every 6 seconds.

A new plastic lens was installed in 1990 when the light was converted to solar power. The Dukes County Historical Society did major work to refurbish the light in 1995. Over time sand gradually filled in the area between the lighthouse and the mainland so that today Edgartown Harbor light is on a beach.

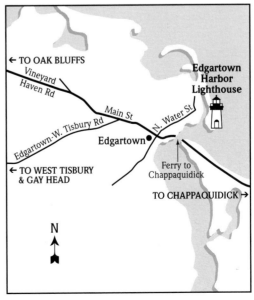

Directions:

Follow signs to Edgartown (via Vineyard Haven Rd. or West Tisbury-Edgartown Rd.) From Main Street in Edgartown turn left (north) onto North Water Street and continue to past the Chappaquiddick Ferry landing. The lighthouse is at the tip of a sandy beach area and marina. Edgartown is a congested area and street parking is often difficult; the lighthouse is a short walk from most anywhere in town.

97

Cape Poge Light

Cape Poge is a windswept point at the northeast tip of Chappaquiddick, an island immediately east of Martha's Vineyard. This lighthouse runs a close second to Nantucket's Brant Point as the New England lighthouse rebuilt and relocated the most times. At least five towers have been built at this location and there have been several moves.

The first 35-foot wooden Cape Poge Lighthouse was built in 1801; the tower exhibited a fixed white light 55 feet above sea level. Although records indicate some sort of previous beacon at the site, little is known of it. President Thomas Jefferson appointed Thomas Mayhew the first keeper at Cape Poge, where he and nine other family members lived for 34 years. After Mayhew's death in

1834 his successor couldn't reach the station for two weeks due to ice. During that time a schooner was wrecked on Cape Poge, claiming several lives.

In 1838 a new tower was built further back from the edge of the eroding bluff but by 1844 its poor condition required that a new tower be constructed. A fourth-order Fresnel lens was added in 1857.

By 1878 the keeper's house was threatened by the sea; a new, larger house was built and a new lighthouse constructed in 1880. A new wooden tower, 40 feet inland from the old one, was built in 1893. Although intended as a temporary structure, that tower is still standing.

CAPE POGE LIGHT, CHAPPAQUID, EDGARTOWN, MASS.

C.1934

The 1893 tower has been relocated four times, first in 1907, then again in 1922. In 1960 the structure was moved back 150 feet and finally, in 1987, moved 500 feet inland by helicopter. At that time a modern plastic lens was installed and repairs made.

In 1943 the light was automated and the last keeper, Joseph Dubois, was removed. The keeper's house was sold to private ownership in 1954 and was subsequently torn down for the lumber. Repairs to the tower were undertaken in 1997.

The lighthouse is a five-mile 'round trip walk over sand from the entrance to the Cape Poge area or four wheel drive vehicle is required.

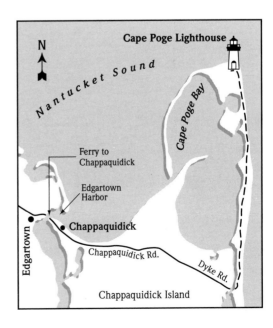

Directions:

In Edgartown take North Water Street to the Chappaquiddick Ferry. The "On Time" ferry departs every 10 minutes daily from June through mid-October, 7:30AM to midnight. The crossing takes 5 minutes; the ferry takes 3 cars, 50 passengers. On Chappaquiddick, follow Chappaquiddick Rd., then Dike Rd. to Cape Poge, the northeast point of Chappaquiddick Island. The route to the lighthouse is 2.5 miles over sand from the entrance to Cape Poge. Four wheel drive is required; the walk takes about one hour each way and is strenuous.

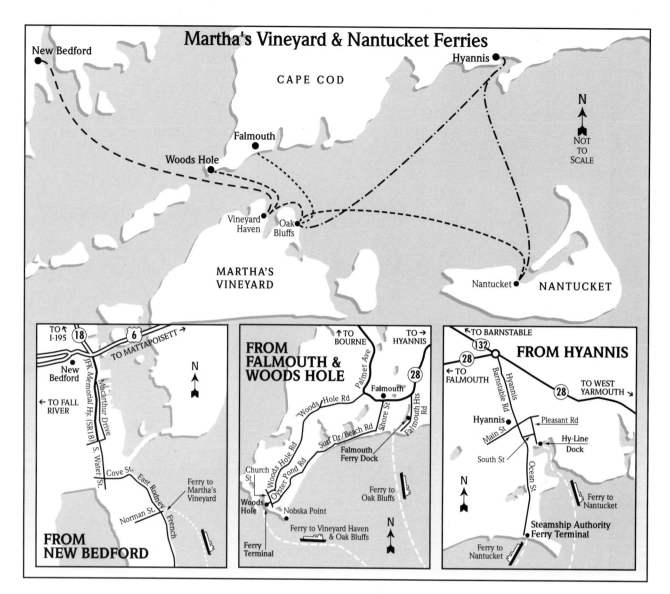

MARTHA'S VINEYARD FERRIES

From Woods Hole: From MA 28 (Palmer Ave.) in Falmouth, turn onto Woods Hole Rd., following the signs to "Vineyard Ferry". Turn left, crossing the bridge to the Woods Hole parking lot and ferry terminal. There is a parking area on Palmer Street if the Woods Hole lot is full (a sign will so indicate); there is shuttle bus service to the ferry. Reservations are required for an automobile. The Woods Hole ferry operates year 'round to Vineyard Haven and Oak Bluffs; crossing time is 45 minutes. **Martha's Vineyard & Nantucket Steamship Authority, P.O. Box 284, Woods Hole, MA 02543 (508) 693- 9130** For automobile reservations: **(508) 477-8600**

From Falmouth: Follow MA 28 into Falmouth (MA 28 is Main St.). Turn south onto Falmouth Heights Road; the ferry dock is about 0.25 mile, just south of Robbins Rd. The Falmouth Ferry operates to Oak Bluffs from late May to mid-October; crossing time is 45 minutes. **Island Commuter Corp. 75 Falmouth Heights Rd., Falmouth, MA 02540 (508) 548-4800.**

**Ferry service to Martha's Vineyard is also available from Hyannis and New Bedford. Both operate only seasonally mid May to late October.

NANTUCKET FERRIES

Ferry transportation to Nantucket is available from Hyannis and Woods Hole. In Hyannis the Hy-Line Cruise dock is on Ocean Street; the Steamship Authority ferry terminal is off South St. just past Pleasant St. Both companies offer parking and private lots also are available nearby. Departure times for both ferries allow sufficient time on the island to visit the lighthouses, but taking a car to the island is not advised. **Hy-Line Cruises, Ocean St. Dock, Hyannis, MA. 02601 (508) 778-2600 (information) (508) 778-2602 (reservations). Steamship Authority: P.O. Box 284 Woods Hole, MA 02543 Reservations: (508)- 477-8600 Information: (508) 228-0262**

Brant Point Light

Brant Point is America's second oldest lighthouse station. The tower has been moved and rebuilt more times than any other with the present lighthouse at least the eighth in this location.

At a town meeting in January of 1746, the merchants and mariners of the town voted to erect a lighthouse at Brant Point to mark the point around which all vessels must pass when entering the island's inner harbor. Keeping of the first light was left to the ship owners.

The first wooden lighthouse burned after 12 years; the second, also made of wood, was destroyed in a storm in March, 1774 and the third by fire in 1783. A fourth light, a makeshift lantern affair, burned in 1786 and the fifth lighthouse lasted only two years before being destroyed by a storm. The next (sixth) lighthouse was ceded to the federal government in 1795. In 1825 a new Brant Point light (seventh) was built with the tower situated atop the keeper's house but the wooden structure fell into disrepair by the 1850s. Finally the eighth light was built, a 47-foot brick tower and brick keeper's house, at a cost of $15,000. The tower received a fourth-order Fresnel lens showing fixed red light.

(Continued, following page)

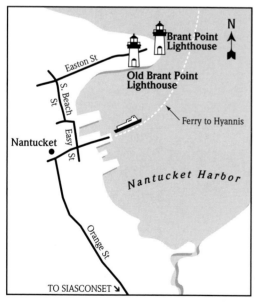

Directions:

From the ferry landing at Nantucket, turn left(west) onto Easy Street and continue to the intersection with Eaton St. Turn right (north) and continue to the streets end at the Coast Guard station and old Brant Point light. The active Brant Point light is at the beach; parking is available on Eaton just before the Coast Guard station.

Old Brant Point Light Station

Because of shifts in the channel, the 1856 light was discontinued in 1900. However, the lighthouse still stands (minus the lantern room), **west** of the present Brant Point Light; it is part of a Coast Guard communications station. The present Brant Point light was built in 1901 and fitted with a fifth-order Fresnel lens. The 13,000 candlepower flashing red light is 26 feet above sea level, making it the lowest of all New England lights. Brant Point is located at the ferry landing.

Sankaty Head Light

A lighthouse at the most southeastern headland in New England was the third established on Nantucket, an island immersed in the thriving whaling industry. To warn mariners away from the newly discovered Davis South Shoals, Sankaty Head Light was built in 1850 on a 90-foot bluff and equipped with a second-order Fresnel lens. The brick and granite lighthouse was the first in Massachusetts to have such a lens with 1/2-inch thick lantern glass to guard against storms and wayward birds.

Sankaty soon became known as New England's most powerful light, reportedly visible for 40 miles.

Nantucket, Mass. - Sankaty Light

Sankaty Head Light also soon became a popular attraction on the island. The keepers were forced to make accommodations to the styles of the day --the small opening to the lantern room had to be enlarged to allow women with hoop skirts to pass through. In 1886 telephone and telegraph lines reached the lighthouse and in 1887 a new, larger keeper's house was constructed.

The light was electrified in 1933; five years later the old clockwork mechanism that turned the lens was replaced by a modern motor. The keeper's house was replaced by a ranch-style dwelling in the late 1930s. After 100 years in the lighthouse, the Fresnel lens was removed in 1950 and rotating aerobeacons installed. The old lens is now located at the Nantucket Whaling Museum. In 1970 the Coast Guard removed the lantern room, but complaints from residents and visitors soon followed and a new aluminum lantern room, similar in appearance to the old one, was installed.

An estimate by the Army Corps of Engineers in 1990 predicted Sankaty Head Light would be in danger of falling over the eroding bluff within 10 years. In 1991, concerned islanders formed a nonprofit group to raise funds for the relocation of the tower. However, during recent years erosion control measures have been successful, delaying the inevitable move or extinction of the lighthouse. Renovations to the tower were done in 1994 but the house and other outbuildings have been removed.

Directions:

From Nantucket Center, follow the signs "To Airport, Siasconset". At the rotary, continue onto Milestone St (follow "To Siasconset" directionals). Follow this road about 8 miles to the village and a small rotary. Continue around the rotary, bearing left into Main St. At the street's end, turn left onto what becomes Sankaty Ave. Turn right onto Butterfly Lane, then left at the T-intersection with Baxter St; the lighthouse is at the end of Baxter St. There is limited parking and the area is thickly settled.

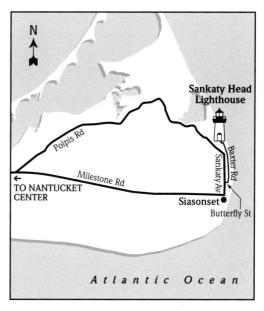

Great Point Light

Before the completion of the Cape Cod Canal in 1914, the stretch between Great Point and Monomoy was one of the busiest sections of the Atlantic coast. The residents of Nantucket first petitioned for a lighthouse in 1770, but not until 1784 did the General Court of Massachusetts agree to the request. The first wooden tower was completed in that same year.For almost 30 years there was no keeper's house at Great Point, so the keepers had to reach the station on foot or horseback, a distance of seven miles. In 1812 a dwelling was constructed but in 1816 the original lighthouse was destroyed by fire. A new stone tower was completed in 1818.

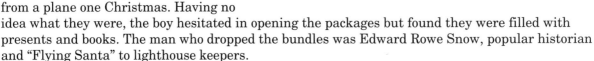

In 1857 Great Point light was fitted with a Fresnel lens, the tower lined with brick and an assistant keeper's house built. Despite the improved light, between 1863 and 1890 there were 43 shipwrecks near the lighthouse; confusion of Great Point light with the Cross Rip lightship was cited.

The son of the last keeper at Great Point remembered seeing packages dropped from a plane one Christmas. Having no idea what they were, the boy hesitated in opening the packages but found they were filled with presents and books. The man who dropped the bundles was Edward Rowe Snow, popular historian and "Flying Santa" to lighthouse keepers.

*"The lighthouse was not sold,
It was very, very old.
This is the new one,
It shines like the sun.
It is located near a bush,
The old one got smushed."*

**Ten-year old student in
Nantucket Elementary School**

106

Great Point light was automated in the 1950s, and in 1968 the keeper's house razed by a suspicious fire, leaving the old stone tower alone at the site. Erosion brought the sea perilously close to the lighthouse and in 1984 a severe storm destroyed the structure, leaving pile of rubble.

Federal money was allocated for building of a new Great Point light; in 1986 a replica, 300 yards west of the old tower, was completed at a cost of more than one million dollars (more than 200 times the cost of the original 1818 tower). The new solar-powered light is visible for 12 miles. Great Point is now part of Coatue Wildlife Refuge and much of the area is off limits. There is an access fee and four-wheel drive vehicle required for the seven-mile over sand route.

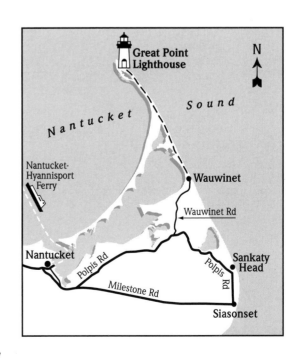

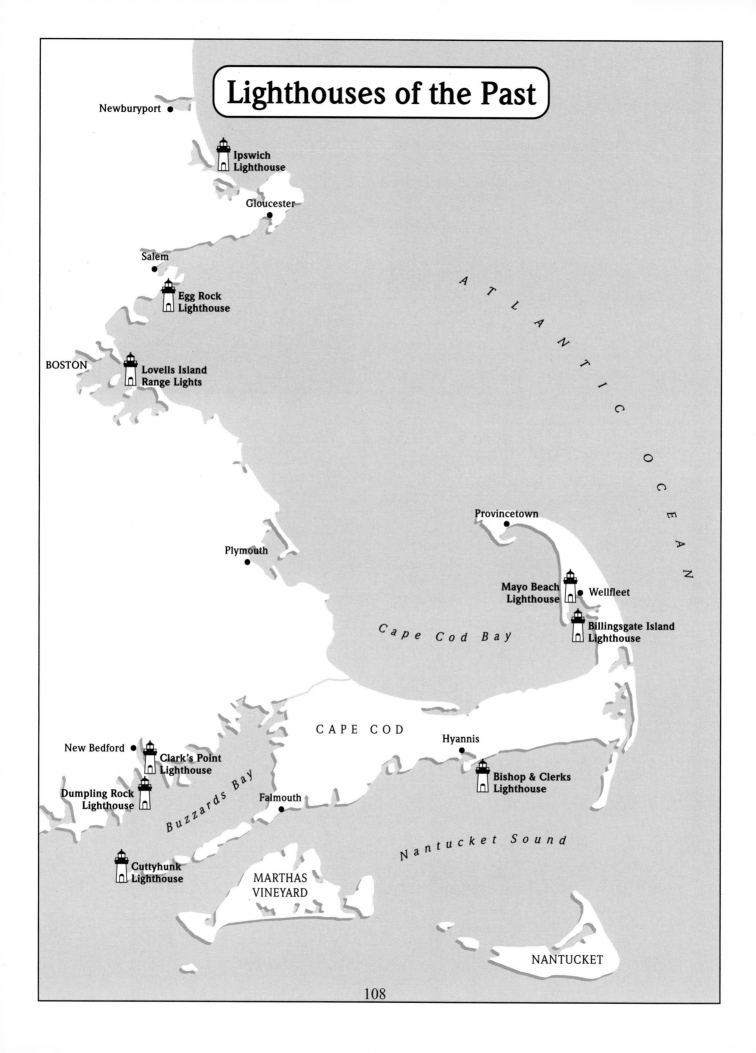

Lighthouses of the Past

Newburyport •

Ipswich
Lighthouse

Gloucester •

Salem •

Egg Rock
Lighthouse

BOSTON

Lovells Island
Range Lights

A T L A N T I C   O C E A N

Provincetown •

Plymouth •

Mayo Beach
Lighthouse • Wellfleet

Billingsgate Island
Lighthouse

C a p e   C o d   B a y

CAPE COD

Hyannis •

New Bedford • Clark's Point
Lighthouse

Dumpling Rock
Lighthouse

Bishop & Clerks
Lighthouse

B u z z a r d s   B a y Falmouth •

N a n t u c k e t   S o u n d

Cuttyhunk
Lighthouse

MARTHAS
VINEYARD

NANTUCKET

Bishop and Clerks Light

Bishops and Clerks light was built in 1858 to mark the dangerous group of rocks known as Bishop and Clerks in Nantucket Sound off Hyannis. Earlier a lightship had been stationed in the vicinity but it was decided a lighthouse would be more practical.

The building of the lighthouse was a difficult process, similar to Massachusetts' Minots Ledge or England's Eddystone. Granite blocks were cut onshore and ferried to the site, then pieced together on a granite foundation. The new 65-foot tower, which stood in open water, replaced nearby Point Gammon light and received a fourth-order Fresnel lens. Keepers worked 20 days at the station, followed by 10 days off; supplies were delivered monthly.

Bishop and Clerks was automated in 1923, then discontinued in 1928. The sea's battering and vandalism took their toll as did a severe storm in 1935. By 1952 the tower tilted to one side and many blocks were missing. The Coast Guard razed the structure; hundred of onlookers in pleasure crafts watched as a dynamite blast toppled the lighthouse. Today a 30-foot pyramidal day beacon marks the spot where the lighthouse once stood; several buoys also warn mariners away from the shoals guarded by Bishops and Clerks for nearly a century.

Dumpling Rock Light

The lighthouse at Dumpling Rock was built in 1828 to help mariners avoid the ledges off Round Hill Point heading toward New Bedford harbor. Originally the lighthouse was a Cape-Cod style with the lantern room on the roof. The sea often encroached on the light station until the government built a wall around Dumpling Rock.

In 1890 a new lighthouse was built, this time a square wooden tower attached to a keeper's house; the lantern room housed a fourth-order Fresnel lens. A new wall was built around the station using stones from the previous keeper's house for a portion of the construction.

Octave Ponsart was keeper during the Hurricane of 1938, the worst in New England history. He and his family were about to leave for vacation when the winds suddenly picked up and seas rose. Ponsart, his assistant and their families fled to an upstairs bedroom, leaving the station's dog, Rexeena, swimming on the first floor. A huge piece of Dumpling Rock itself was torn away by the storm and crashed through the living room wall. The boulder stayed in place, partly inside the dwelling, anchoring the house to the rock. The freak accident likely saved the lives of the keepers and family members; the dog survived as well by climbing to the top shelf of a linen closet.

Repairs were made to the station but damage was extensive. The remains of the lighthouse were removed in 1940 and a skeleton tower was placed at the site.

Billingsgate Island light

In 1620 the Pilgrims on the Mayflower recorded a 60-acre island off Wellfleet, later named Billingsgate after a great London fishmarket. Today the island is remembered as Cape Cod's Atlantis.

A small brick lighthouse, 14 feet tall and 45 feet above sea level, was built in 1822 at the island's southern tip; a keeper's house also was constructed. By the mid-nineteenth century Billingsgate had a community of 30 homes, a school and fish oil plant. The lighthouse was, in 1855, already being threatened by the sea. Therefore, in 1858 a new structure, similar to the first, was built further north. That lighthouse too was soon threatened. In an attempt to delay the inevitable, the Lighthouse Board in 1888 built 1000 feet of jetties and bulkheads around the island.

By 1915 the population of the island was only two: the lighthouse keeper and a watchman who guarded the oyster bed. The lens and lamp were removed from the lighthouse, which toppled in a storm the day after Christmas. A skeleton tower was erected but that light was finally discontinued in 1922; by 1942 the island had completely disappeared. Today Billingsgate shoal is marked by a buoy.

Cuttyhunk Light

The first lighthouse on three-mile long Cuttyhunk Island (then called "Cutterhunk"), was a 25-foot stone tower built in 1823 to guide vessels entering Buzzard's Bay. Evidently not of sound construction, the structure had to be twice encased in brick. In 1857 a fifth-order Fresnel lens was installed and in 1860 the keeper's house enlarged to two stories; a lantern room was placed on the roof to replace the old lighthouse. A new 45-foot lighthouse was constructed in 1891.

The Hurricane of 1944 hit Cuttyhunk directly, changing the shape of the island located at the far southwestern corner of the Elizabeth Islands off Falmouth. The lighthouse was discontinued in 1947; the structure was torn down and replaced by a skeleton tower. Only a stone oil house remains from the original lighthouse station.

A ferry from New Bedford will take you to Cuttyhunk but there are no remains of the lighthouse tower. Keeper Octave Ponsart is buried on the island and a lighthouse is carved on his gravestone.

Clarks Point Light

A 42-foot stone tower was the first lighthouse built at Clark's Point to guide vessels into New Bedford harbor. In the 1860s a seven-sided granite fort was built next to the light. Because the walls of Fort Taber eventually blocked the view of the light, in 1869 the lantern room and keeper's quarters were relocated to the top of the fort. The old stone light tower stood until it was demolished in 1906. In 1889 a new lighthouse (Butler Flats Light) was built offshore from Clark's Point, making it obsolete. The light atop the fort was discontinued in 1889.

The fort and lighthouse were restored in the 1970s only to fall victim to extensive vandalism and theft. A wastewater treatment facility presently stands next to the fort; the whole site is in a state of disrepair, with the old lighthouse no more than odd pieces of rusting metal.

110

Egg Rock Light

Egg Rock appears to rise like a whale out of the ocean a mile northeast of Nahant, Massachusetts and can be seen from many locations north of Boston. The island is in an unprotected location and is often battered by fierce winds and waves, frequently becoming icebound in winter. The first lighthouse on the island was built in 1856 in response to demands of Swampscott fishermen; the light tower was on top of the keeper's house.

7957 Egg Rock Light, Swampscott, Mass.

C. 1905

The lighthouse burned in 1897 and a similar structure was soon rebuilt. In 1919 it was decided a keeper was no longer needed at Egg Rock and an automatic beacon was placed in the tower; the light was discontinued in 1922. The government offered the lighthouse for $5 to anyone who would pay for removal of the building from the island. A buyer was found and arrangements made for the move. However, a rope snapped during the moving process, sending the lighthouse onto its side then crashing into the ocean. There are no remains of the station.

This station boasted one of the most famous lighthouse pets, Milo, a huge Newfoundland-St. Bernard mix belonging to the first keeper, George Taylor. During an expedition to shoot waterfowl on the island, Milo swam in pursuit of a downed loon. However the loon, not mortally wounded, took flight repeatedly; each time Milo gave chase. Taylor watched the pursuit until the loon and Milo disappeared from sight. The dog was not seen until the next day when, after apparently spending the night in Nahant, he was spotted swimming back to Egg Rock. Milo achieved fame over the next few years as rescuer of several children around the island.

Another tale frequently associated with Egg Rock is that of an 19th century keeper's wife who died in early winter. Unable to take the body to the mainland, the keeper laid her in the oilhouse for the remainder of the winter. In early spring, with clearing of the ice, he rowed his wife's body to the mainland and a funeral was held. After the funeral the keeper visited with a childhood sweetheart, hastily proposed marriage and sought out the same preacher who'd hours before officiated at the funeral. The keeper returned to Egg Rock with a new wife before nightfall.

Lovells Island Range Lights

C. 1909

Lovells Island, about 3/4 mile long and 1/3 mile wide, is about seven miles from Boston and 1.5 miles from Boston light. In 1902 two lighthouses were built at the part of the island called Ram's Head to direct mariners using the South Channel of Broad Sound. The lighthouses were 400 feet apart, 40 and 31 feet tall, with a connecting walkway, keeper's house and oil house.

The French warship *Magnifique* was wrecked on the island in 1782. In 1919 Keeper Charles Jennings dug up some European coins from his garden; he believed them to be from the wrecked ship. Upon returning from leave shortly thereafter, Keeper Jennings found a large hole in his garden. His assitant had just gone on leave and abruptly left the Lighthouse Service, leading some to believe he'd found the rest of the *Magnifique's* treasure.

For years the Lovells Island Range lights shared the island with Fort Standish. To make room for expansion of the fort in the late 1930s, the light station was discontinued. The towers were dismantled in 1939; all that remains is the station's oil shed.

Ipswich Light

Previously an Indian village called Agawam, Ipswich is one of New England's oldest towns, incorparated in 1634. The shellfish industry has long been the lifeblood of the town and range lights were built at Crane's Beach in 1838 to mark the entrance to the busy fishing harbor. The two square brick towers were moved nine times during the next four decades as the channel shifted.

In 1875 the rear range light was replaced by a white cast-iron tower; the front range light was discontinued in 1932 and the rear light automated. In 1939 the rear lighthouse was moved to Edgartown on Martha's Vineyard to replace a structure badly damaged in the Hurricane of 1938. The Ipswich light was replaced by a skeleton tower.

The "Flying Santa" was an integral part of Christmas celebrations for lighthouse families and their children. One year a group of children was gathered at the Ipswich lighthouse in anticipation of his visit. As the scheduled arrival time neared, the keeper asked his wife if Santa had yet arrived. At that very moment there was a crash from upstairs; Santa's package had been delivered on time, made a direct hit on the skylight and landed in the upstairs hallway. The keeper's wife responded appropriately, "Yes, dear, I think we can start the party now."

Mayo Beach Light

A lighthouse on Mayo Beach was intended to aid mariners entering Wellfleet harbor, a busy 19th century fishing port. Completed in 1838, the saltbox-style four-room keeper's house had a lantern room on top with a Fresnel lens added in 1857. A new cast-iron tower and brick and clapboard keeper's dwelling were built in 1881 to replace the previous poorly built structure. The light was discontinued in 1922 and the property passed into private ownership. The house and 1907 oil house remain and are well maintained; the foundation of the lighthouse can be seen adjacent to the house.

LIGHTHOUSE	COLOR	CHARACTERISTICS	DESCRIPTION
Portsmouth Harbor	Green	Flashing	Height above water: 52 ft Range : 12nm
Isles of Shoals	White	Flashing 15 seconds	Height above water: 82 ft Range: 20 nm
Newburyport Range Lights (inactive)	N A	N A	N A
Newburyport Harbor (Plum Is)	Green	Group occulting flashing every 15 seconds	Height above water: 50ft Range: 10nm
Annisquam Harbor	White with red sector	Flashing 7.5 sec with red sector	Height above water: 45 ft Range:White=14,Red=11nm
Straightsmouth Is.	Green	Flashing every 6 seconds	Height above water: 46 ft Range: 6nm
Thachers Is.	White	Flashing, five times at 20-second intervals	Height above water: 124 ft Range: 19 nm
Eastern Point	White	Flashing 5 seconds	Height above water: 57 ft Range: 24 nm
Ten Pound Island	Red	Equal interval, 6 seconds	Height above water: 57 ft Range: 5 nm
Bakers Island	White, red	Flashing, alternating white & red, each 20 seconds	Height above water: 111 ft Range:White=16;Red=13nm
Hospital Point Front Range	White	Fixed	Height above water: 70 ft
Hospital Point Rear Range	White	Fixed	Height above water: 183 ft
Fort Pickering	White	Flashing 4 seconds	Height above water: 28 ft
Derby Wharf	Red	Flashing red 6 seconds	Height above water: 25 ft Range: 4 nm
Marblehead	Green	Fixed	Height above water: 130ft Range: 7 nm
Long Island Head	White	Flashing 2.5 seconds	Height above water: 120 ft Range: 6 nm
Deer Island	Red, white	Alternating red/white flashing 10 seconds with red sector	Height above water: 53 ft Range:white=14;red=10nm
The Graves	White	Flashing, twice each 12 seconds	Height above water: 98 ft Range: 24 nm
Boston	White	Flashing 10 seconds	Height above water: 102 ft Range: 27 nm

LIGHTHOUSE	COLOR	CHARACTERISTICS	DESCRIPTION
Minots Ledge	White	Group flashing, 1-4-3 each 45 seconds	Height above water: 85 ft Range: 10 nm
Scituate	White	Flashing 15 seconds	Height above water: 70 ft.
Plymouth	White, red sector	Group flashing alternate single & double white every 20 sec.- includes red sector	Height above water: 102 ft Range:White=16;Red=14nm
Duxbury Pier	Red	Group red flashing 3 times each 10 seconds	Height above water: 35 ft Range: 6 nm
Cleveland East Ledge	White	Flashing 10 seconds	Height above water: 74 ft Range: 17 nm
Butler Flats	White	Flashing 4 seconds	Height above water: 53 ft Range: 4 nm
Palmers Island	White	Flashing 4 seconds	Height above water: 42ft Range: 5 nm
Ned Point	White	Flashing 6 seconds each 6 seconds	Height above water: 41 ft Range: 12nm
Borden Flats	White	Flashing 2.5 seconds	Height above water: 47 ft Range: 11 nm
Bird Island	White	Flashing 6 seconds	Height above water: Range:
Tarpaulin Cove	White	Flashing 6 seconds	Height above water: 78 ft Range: 9 nm
Wings Neck (inactive)	NA	NA	NA
Sandy Neck (inactive)	NA	NA	NA
Nobska Point	White with red sector	Flashing each 6 seconds	Height above water: 87ft Range:White 16nm;red12nm
Bass River	NA	NA	NA
West Dennis	White	Flashing seconds	Height above water: 44 ft
Point Gammon (inactive)	NA	NA	NA
Stage Harbor (Inactive)	NA	NA	NA
Monomoy Point	NA	NA	NA

LIGHTHOUSE	COLOR	CHARACTERISTICS	DESCRIPTION
Chatham	White	Group flashing white twice each 10 seconds	Height above water:80 ft Range: 24nm
Nauset Beach	Red, white	Alternate red & white lights fl. each 5 sec.	Ht above water:114 ft Range: white 23; red 19nm
Highland	White	Flashing 5 seconds	Height above water: 183 ft Range: 23 nm
Race Point	White	Flashing 10 seconds	Height above water: 41 ft Range: 16 nk
Wood End	Red	Flashing 10 seconds	Height above water: 45 ft Range: 13 nm
Long Point	Green	Flashing	Height above water: 36 ft Range: 8nm
West Chop	White	Occulting 4 seconds with red sector	Height above water: 84 ft Range: White 15, red 11 nm
East Chop	Green	Equal interval each 6 seconds	Height above water: 79 ft Range: 9 nm
Gay Head	White, red	Flashing white alt. with flashing red each 40 seconds	Height above water: 170 ft Range: White 24;red 20nm
Edgartown Harbor	Red	Flashing 6 seconds	Height above water: 45 ft Range: 5 nm
Cape Poge	White	Flashing 6 seconds	Height above water: 65 ft Range: 9 nm
Brant Point	Red	Occulting 4 seconds, lighted 3 seconds	Height above water: 26 ft Range: 10nm
Sankaty Head	White	Flashing 7.5 seconds	Height above water: 158 ft Range: 24 nm
Great Point (Nantucket Light)	White	Flasing white 5 seconds with red sector	Height above water: 71 ft Range:White=14; red 12nm
Portsmouth Harbor (NH)	Green	Fixed	Height above water: 52ft Range: 12nm
Isle of Shoals- NH (White Island)	White	Flashing 15 seconds	Height above water: 82 ft Range: 20nm

Information contained herein not intended for navigational purpose.
Consult appropriate chart data.

Tour and Excursion Boat Information

There are many information and visitor centers which offer brochures and schedules for various tours which include viewing of lighthouses in a particular area. The following is a selected list of tours available; many are added or changed each season.

Cape Ann & Northern Shore

Gloucester:

Tiny Tug Tours: Cap't. George Story, (508)-283-4049. This a tug boat ideally suited to getting in close to lighthouses and the shoreline. Custom lighthouse trips arranged on request.

Ten Pound Is. Shuttle: Water taxi offered to Ten Pound Is. during the summer season; continually makes round trips between the island, Gloucester waterfront and Rocky Neck art colony.

Thacher Is. Association: Overnight stays at Thachers will be resumed when the dock is rebuilt. To contact the association directors regarding progress: P.O. Box 36, Rockport, MA. (508) 546-7697

Cape Ann Lighthouse Cruise: *The Bev,* Harbor Loop, Gloucester (508) 283- 1979

Any of the whale watch trips from Gloucester will pass by Ten Pound Island Eastern Point Lights en route (i.e. **Cape Ann Whale Watch 800-877-5110 , Cap't. Bills Whale Watch (800-33-WHALE)**

Salem Shores and Harbors

Salem:

Whale watches from Salem may pass Baker's en route to the feeding grounds. Most tour boats from Salem will pass Ft. Pickering (Winter Is.) Light and Derby Wharf Light and many include Marblehead and Hospital Point Lights.

East India Cruise Co. , 197 Derby St., Salem, MA. (508) 744-8718

Boston Harbor

Boston:

Friends of Boston Harbor Islands--offers several trips during the season to Boston Light (including landing on the island with about 1-2 hours to visit the grounds and tower. The group also offers other lighthouse trips to the north and south shore(s) which may include up to 6-8 lighthouses per trip. Specific routes vary each season. Call for information and trip schedules: **(617) 740-4290**

Boston Harbor Explorers--also offers cruises to view the lights in Boston Harbor and beyond. Trip schedules and routes vary seasonally; call for information **P.O. Box 744, Quincy, MA. (617) 479-1871**

Friends of Flying Santa--also offers some trips to the Boston Harbor lights and others along the north and south shores. Specialty trips also offered as demand warrants (i.e. to view the offshore lights of New Hampshire) **P.O. Box 791, Hull, MA. 02045 (617) 925-0783**

Boston Harbor Cruises-- One Long Wharf, Boston, MA. (617) 227-4321

Massachusetts Bay Lines--60 Rowes Wharf, Boston, MA. (617) 542-8000

Cruises to Provincetown and the whale watches will pass Deer Island and Long Island Head Lights en route; others may be visible distantly.

South Shore

Plymouth:

Harbor tours from Plymouth will pass fairly close to Duxbury Pier light and The Gurnet Light. The ferry to Provincetown also passes these lights en route.

Cap't. John Boats/ Cape Cod Cruises (at the town wharf) **(800) 242-2469**

To view **Minot's Ledge Light**: Contact Friends of Boston Harbor Islands, Boston Harbor Explorers or Friends of Flying Santa. These groups try to include Minots in at least one trip per season but sea conditions are extremely variable and often preclude close viewing or require alternate route.

Southeastern Shore

There are no harbor tours in New Bedford or Fall River or most other towns with lighthouses in their area. The ferry from New Bedford to Martha's Vineyard passes close by Butler Flats Light **(508) 997-1688**

The Audubon Society makes regular trips to Bird Is. (off Marion, MA) to check the terns on the island. The Bird Is. Preservation Society hopes to offer increased access now that the light is again lighted.

Cape Cod

Woods Hole/Falmouth:

Ferries to Martha's Vineyard pass Nobska Light.

Hyannis/Hyannisport:

The ferry to Nantucket passes the So. Hyannis Light, and Pt. Gammon light, but distantly. Catamaran trips from Hyannisport will offer closer views of Pt. Gammon if requested. **(Catboat Rides, (508)775-0222)**

Barnstable:

Whale watches leaving from Barnstable pass Sandy Neck Light en route. **Hyannis Whale Watcher, P.O. Box 254, Barnstable, MA. 800-287-0374**

Cape Cod Museum of Natural History:

Offers day and overnight trips to Monomoy Island during the season, **P.O. Box 1710, Brewster, MA. (800) 479-3867.** The Audubon Society also offers trips to the island out of Wellfleet; while primarily geared to birding, there is opportunity to break from the group to visit the lighthouse. Sea conditions determine suitability for landing with both groups.

Provincetown:

There are boat shuttles available to Long Point during the season.
(Flyer's, 134A Commercial St., 800-750-0898)
Whale watches also pass by Wood End, Long Point and Race Point Lights as to the Provincetown/ Gloucester Ferries

Chatham:

Chatham Harbor Tours (at the fish pier); **(508) 255-0619**

Martha's Vineyard & Nantucket

Martha's Vineyard:

Ferries from Woods Hole and Falmouth pass West Chop or East Chop Lights, depending on whether arriving in Vineyard Haven or Oak Bluffs.

Edgartown--the "On Time" ferry to Chappaquiddick offers a view of the Edgartown Harbor Light from the water (carries passengers and three cars per trip).

There are numerous tours available which take in all Vineyard lights except Cape Poge.

Nantucket:

The ferries from Hyannisport and Harwichport dock just "next door" to the Brant Point Lighthouse and passes directly by it on entry to the harbor. **(Steamship Authority (508) 477-8600 or Hy-Line Cruises (508) 778-2600**

Flights to and from Hyannis to Nantucket afford views of Pt. Gammon Light (on Great Island near Hyannis), Brant Point and Gt.Point Lights en route. **(Island Airlines, 800-248-7779 or Cape Air 800-352-0714**

There are a variety of tour vans available on Nantucket which will include Brant Point and Sankaty Head Light **(Ara's Tours (508) 228-1951, Island Tours (508) 228-0334**

Four-wheel drive jeeps are available for rent at **Windmill Auto Rental** (at the airport)**(800) 228-1227** or from **Young's Bicycle Rental** at the ferry dock

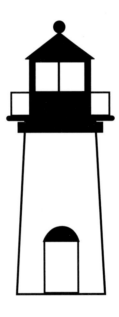

Organizations

All groups listed are involved in lighthouse preservation, restoration, repair and maintenance with donations/membership dues going to these efforts. Some offer regular or seasonal trips to the light(s). Most are nonprofit organizations and all welcome contributions.

Bird Island Light: Bird Island Preservation Society, 2 Spring St., Marion, MA 02738 **(508) 748-0550**

Boston Harbor:
> Friends of Boston Harbor Islands: **(617) 740-4290**
> Boston Harbor Explorers: P.O. Box 744 Quincy, MA **(617) 479-1871**

Butler Flats Light: City of New Bedford (Housing & Community Development), 133 William St., Rm 208, New Bedford, MA. 02740

Derby Wharf Light: National Park Service, Salem Nat'l. Historic Site, 174 Derby St., Salem, MA.. 01970

East Chop, Gay Head Lights: Dukes County Historical Society, Box 827, Edgartown, MA. 02539 **(508) 627-4441**

Highland Light: Truro Historical Society, Inc.P.O. Box 486, Truro, MA. **(508) 487-3397**

Race Point, Long Point and Wood End Lights: Cape Cod Chapter of the New England Lighthouse Foundation, P.O. Box 1690, Wells, ME. 04090

Monomoy Light (trips): Cape Cod Museum of Natural History, P.O. Box 1710, Brewster, MA. **(508) 896-3867**

Nauset Light: Nauset Light Preservation Society, P.O. Box 941, Eastham, MA. 02642

Plum Island (Newburyport Harbor) Light: Friends of Plum Island, Inc., P.O. Box 381, Newburyport, MA. 01950

Scituate Light: Scituate Historical Society, Scituate, MA. 02066 **(617) 545-1083**

Thachers Island Lights: Thacher Island Association, P.O. Box 73, Rockport, MA 01966

U.S. Lighthouse Society: 244 Kearny St., 5th Floor, San Francisco, CA. 94108. Offers a Cape Cod trip, includes viewing lighthouses en route from Provincetown to Gloucester. Write for membership information and tour dates.

Index

Annisquam Light

CatNap Publications
P.O. Box 848
Mt. Desert, ME. 04660